MOJO PROGRAMMING THE FAST TRACK TO MASTERING ROBOTIC PROCESS AUTOMATION

THE COMPLETE GUIDE

WILLIAM K ROBERT

Copyright © 2024 by WILLIAM K ROBERT

All rights reserved. No part of this publication may be reproduced, distributed, or transmitted in any form or by any means, including photocopying, recording, or other electronic or mechanical methods, without the prior written permission of the publisher, except in the case of brief quotations embodied in critical reviews and certain other non commercial uses permitted by copyright law.

CONTENTS

Chapter 1: Introduction to Robotic Process Automation (RPA)

1.1 Robotic Process Automation (RPA) Explained

1.2 The Compelling Advantages of RPA: Cost Savings, Accuracy, and Employee Redeployment

1.3 Identifying Automation Goldmines: A Framework for RPA Opportunities

1.4 Mojo: The RPA Developer's Power Tool

Chapter 2: Getting Started with Mojo Programming

2.1 Setting Up Your Mojo Development Environment

2.2 Grasping the Mojo Syntax - Building Blocks for Automation

2.3 Mastery over Data: Variables and Data Types in Mojo

2.4 Your First Steps in Mojo Programming - Building a Simple Program

Chapter 3: Mastering Mojo Control Flow

3.1 Taking Control with Conditionals: if/else in Mojo

3.2 Conquering Repetition with Loops: for and while in Mojo

3.3 Safeguarding Your Programs: Error Handling in Mojo

3.4 Unveiling the Mystery: Debugging Your Mojo Programs

Chapter 4: Working with Data in Mojo

4.1 Taming the Data: Manipulation Techniques in Mojo

4.2 Conquering Data Sources: Extracting and Handling Information

4.3 Shaping the Data: Formatting and Transformation for Automation

4.4 Safeguarding Your Data: Validation Techniques in Mojo

Chapter 5: Mojo for User Interface (UI) Automation

5.1 Mastering the GUI: Automating Desktop Applications with Mojo

5.2 Conquering the Web: Automating Browser Interactions with Mojo

5.3 Crafting Enduring Automation: Best Practices for Robust UI Automation Scripts in Mojo

Chapter 6: Leveraging Mojo for File and Folder Management

6.1 Taming the Filesystem: Automating File Operations with Mojo

6.2 Conquering the Folderscape: Organizing and Managing Directories with Mojo

6.3 Embracing Diversity: Working with Various File Formats in Mojo

6.4 Uploading and Downloading with Ease: Automating File Transfers in Mojo

Chapter 7: Integrating Mojo with Other Tools and Technologies

7.1 Bridging the Gap: Connecting Mojo to Databases and APIs

7.2 Expanding Horizons: Enhancing Mojo Programs with External Libraries

7.3 Automation on Autopilot: Triggering Mojo Scripts with Schedulers

7.4 Conquering the Climb: Building Scalable RPA Solutions with Mojo

Chapter 8: Advanced Mojo Programming Techniques

8.1 Mastering the Unexpected: Advanced Exception Handling in Mojo

8.2 Mastering Patterns: Unleashing the Power of Regular Expressions in Mojo

8.3 Building Blocks of Automation: Reusable Components and Functions in Mojo

8.4 Mastering the Craft: Best Practices for Efficient Mojo Development

Chapter 9: Deploying and Maintaining Your Mojo RPA Solutions

9.1 Sharing the Automation Power: Packaging and Deploying Mojo Robots

9.2 Keeping an Eye on the Automation: Monitoring and Logging for Mojo Robots

9.3 Safeguarding the Automation: Security Best Practices for RPA

9.4 Keeping Track of Changes: Version Control and Collaboration for Mojo Projects

Chapter 10: The Future of Mojo and RPA

10.1 A Glimpse into the Future: Emerging Trends in RPA.

10.2 The Power of Two: AI and RPA - A Synergistic Force

10.3 Your Path to Automation Expertise: Building a Career in RPA

10.4 Keeping Your Mojo Flowing: Staying Up-to-Date with the Latest Advancements

Chapter 1: Introduction to Robotic Process Automation (RPA)

1.1 Robotic Process Automation (RPA) Explained

Robotic Process Automation (RPA) is a technology that utilizes software robots to automate repetitive, rule-based tasks traditionally performed by humans. These software robots, often called bots, mimic human actions by interacting with digital systems and applications.

Here's a breakdown of how RPA automates tasks:

1. Defining the Task and Workflow:

Business analysts and process owners identify repetitive tasks that are well-defined and follow clear rules. This could involve tasks like data entry, processing invoices, or generating reports.

2. Building the Software Robot:

RPA developers use tools to design the software robot (bot). This involves defining the steps the bot will take, including:

-Accessing specific applications and data sources.

-Extracting and manipulating data.

-Performing actions like typing, clicking buttons, and navigating menus.

-Following decision-making logic based on predefined rules.

3. Execution and Monitoring:

-The software robot runs the defined workflow autonomously. It interacts with the applications as a human user would, but with increased speed and accuracy.

-RPA tools often provide monitoring and logging functionalities. This allows users to track the robot's performance, identify errors, and ensure smooth operation.

Benefits of RPA:

Increased Efficiency: Automating repetitive tasks frees up human employees to focus on more strategic work.

Improved Accuracy: RPA eliminates errors caused by human data entry and ensures consistent task execution.

Reduced Costs: Automating tasks can lead to significant cost savings in terms of labor and operational expenses.

Enhanced Scalability: RPA solutions can handle high volumes of data and transactions effortlessly.

Analogy: RPA in Action

Imagine an employee spends hours copying and pasting data between spreadsheets or filling out forms with repetitive information. RPA can automate this process by creating a software bot that acts like a tireless assistant:

-The bot opens the relevant spreadsheets.

-It extracts the required data from specific cells.

-The bot then opens the application for data entry.

-It accurately types the extracted data into the designated fields.

-The bot can even submit the completed forms electronically.

In essence, RPA automates the "how" of a task, allowing humans to focus on the "why" and "what" - the strategic thinking and decision-making aspects of the job.

1.2 The Compelling Advantages of RPA: Cost Savings, Accuracy, and Employee Redeployment

Robotic Process Automation (RPA) offers a compelling value proposition for businesses seeking to streamline operations, improve efficiency, and reduce costs. Here's a closer look at three key benefits of implementing RPA solutions:

1. Cost Savings:

Reduced Labor Costs: RPA automates repetitive tasks that were previously performed by human employees. This can lead to significant cost savings in terms of salaries, benefits, and training expenses.

Improved Operational Efficiency: Automating workflows eliminates time wasted on repetitive tasks, allowing employees to complete tasks faster and with fewer errors. This translates to increased productivity and overall operational efficiency.

Reduced Errors and Rework: Human error is a major contributor to rework and wasted resources in manual processes. RPA eliminates this risk by performing tasks with perfect accuracy and consistency. This reduces the need for rework and associated costs.

Example: Consider a scenario where a company employs several data entry clerks to process invoices. Implementing RPA for data entry can significantly reduce the number of employees needed, leading to substantial cost savings.

2. Improved Accuracy and Efficiency:

Elimination of Human Error: Repetitive data entry and manual tasks are prone to errors like typos, missed data points, and inconsistencies. RPA eliminates these errors by following predefined rules and logic, ensuring accurate data processing and task execution.

Increased Processing Speed: Software robots can perform tasks much faster than humans. This significantly reduces processing times for high-volume tasks, leading to faster turnaround times and improved overall efficiency.

Enhanced Compliance: RPA ensures consistent and accurate execution of tasks, which is crucial for adhering to industry regulations and internal compliance requirements.

Example: Automating data extraction from various sources for financial reporting can ensure accurate and timely reports, leading to better decision-making and improved financial compliance.

3. Freeing Up Human Employees for Higher-Value Work:

Focus on Strategic Activities: By automating repetitive tasks, RPA allows human employees to dedicate their time and skills to more strategic and value-added activities. This could involve tasks like:

-Customer service interaction and relationship building

-Data analysis and generating insights

-Process improvement and innovation

-Project management and problem-solving

Increased Employee Satisfaction: Automating mundane tasks can improve employee morale and satisfaction. Employees can utilize their skills for more engaging and challenging work, leading to increased motivation and job fulfillment.

Example: Imagine a team of customer service representatives spending a significant portion of their day processing routine inquiries. Automating these inquiries with RPA frees them up to handle complex customer issues and build stronger customer relationships.

In conclusion, RPA offers a win-win situation for both businesses and employees. By automating repetitive tasks, businesses can achieve significant cost savings, improve accuracy and efficiency, and empower employees to focus on more valuable work.

1.3 Identifying Automation Goldmines: A Framework for RPA Opportunities

Robotic Process Automation (RPA) shines brightest when applied to the right tasks. Here, we'll explore a framework for identifying tasks ripe for RPA implementation and strategies for analyzing workflows to uncover these automation opportunities.

The RPA Suitability Framework:

RPA thrives on automating tasks that meet these core criteria:

Repetitive and Rule-Based: Tasks involving repetitive steps and following clear, well-defined rules are ideal for RPA. These tasks often lack complexity and require minimal human judgment.

High Volume: Processes that involve a high volume of data or transactions can benefit significantly from automation. RPA can handle large datasets with speed and consistency, freeing up human resources.

Error-Prone: Tasks susceptible to human error due to repetitive data entry or manipulation are prime candidates for RPA.

Automating these tasks eliminates errors and ensures consistent, accurate execution.

Stable Processes: Processes that are well-defined and don't change frequently are easier to automate effectively. Frequent changes can require frequent updates to the RPA solution, impacting its efficiency.

Unearthing Automation Gems: Analyzing Workflows

Now that we have the criteria, how do we find these tasks within our workflows? Here are some strategies:

Process Mapping: Visually map out the steps involved in a process. Identify repetitive tasks, decision points, and data manipulation steps. Look for opportunities to automate sequences of repetitive steps with clear rules.

Time and Motion Studies: Analyze how much time employees spend on specific tasks within a process. Tasks with a high percentage of time dedicated to repetitive actions are good candidates for RPA.

Employee Interviews: Talk to employees who perform the tasks. Get their insights on repetitive aspects, challenges, and areas where automation could be beneficial.

Focus on Bottlenecks: Identify bottlenecks or slowdowns within a workflow. If these involve repetitive tasks with clear rules, RPA can potentially streamline the process and improve overall efficiency.

Putting it into Practice:

Imagine a scenario where the accounts payable department spends a significant amount of time processing invoices. Here's how to identify potential automation opportunities:

Process Mapping: Map out the invoice processing steps, including data entry, verification, and approval. You might identify repetitive tasks like data entry from invoices into the accounting system.

Employee Interviews: Talk to accounts payable staff. They might highlight challenges with data entry accuracy and the time-consuming nature of the task.

Based on the RPA suitability framework and workflow analysis, automating data entry from invoices into the accounting system appears promising. This task is repetitive, involves high data volume, and follows clear rules, making it a strong candidate for RPA implementation.

By following this framework and employing these analysis strategies, you can effectively identify tasks within your organization that are best suited for RPA, paving the way for a more automated and efficient future.

1.4 Mojo: The RPA Developer's Power Tool

Robotic Process Automation (RPA) development requires a language that's both powerful and user-friendly. Here's where Mojo shines. This section explores how Mojo's design caters specifically to RPA development and the advantages it offers over other programming languages in this domain.

Built for the RPA Arena:

Mojo is a programming language specifically designed with RPA development in mind. It incorporates features that streamline the process of automating user interactions and workflows:

Simplified Syntax: Mojo borrows from languages like Python, offering a clean and easy-to-learn syntax. This allows developers, even those with limited programming experience, to quickly pick up Mojo and start building RPA solutions.

Focus on User Interactions: Mojo provides built-in functions and libraries specifically designed for interacting with various applications and user interfaces (UIs). This eliminates the need for developers to write complex code from scratch for simulating clicks, keystrokes, and other user actions.

Data Manipulation Capabilities: Mojo offers robust functionalities for data manipulation, parsing, and transformation. This is essential for handling data extracted from different sources during RPA workflows.

Integration with External Systems: Mojo can integrate with various databases, APIs, and other external systems. This allows RPA solutions to interact with existing IT infrastructure and exchange data seamlessly.

Mojo's Edge over the Competition:

While other programming languages can be used for RPA development, Mojo offers distinct advantages:

Ease of Use: Compared to languages like C++ or Java, Mojo's simpler syntax and focus on RPA-specific functionalities make it easier and faster to develop RPA solutions.

Visual Development Tools (if applicable): Some RPA platforms offer visual development tools that allow building workflows using drag-and-drop functionality and pre-built components. While some general-purpose languages might require extensive coding, Mojo can potentially benefit from such visual tools within RPA platforms for faster development.

Focus on Automating User Interactions: Mojo's built-in functionalities for UI interaction simplify the process of automating tasks that involve interacting with various applications and desktops. This can be more cumbersome to achieve in general-purpose languages.

In essence, Mojo bridges the gap between complex programming and user-friendly automation development. Its design specifically caters to the needs of RPA developers, making it a powerful tool for building efficient and scalable RPA solutions.

Note: The inclusion of "visual development tools (if applicable)" depends on the specific RPA platforms that integrate with Mojo. This chapter provides a general overview, and future chapters might delve deeper into specific RPA platforms and their potential integration with Mojo for a more holistic understanding.

Chapter 2: Getting Started with Mojo Programming

2.1 Setting Up Your Mojo Development Environment

Choosing Your Development Playground:

There are several ways to develop Mojo programs. Here's a quick overview of the most common options:

Integrated Development Environments (IDEs): IDEs like Visual Studio Code or PyCharm offer a comprehensive development environment with features like code completion, debugging tools, and syntax highlighting. These can significantly enhance your development experience. Some IDEs might even have plugins specifically designed for Mojo development, providing additional functionalities.

Standalone Text Editors: Simpler text editors like Sublime Text or Notepad++ can also be used for Mojo development. While they lack the advanced features of IDEs, they can be a good starting point, especially for smaller projects.

Online Playgrounds: Some online platforms offer Mojo playgrounds where you can write and run Mojo code directly in your web browser. This is a convenient option for trying out code snippets or learning the basics without installing any software.

Installing the Mojo SDK:

Here's a step-by-step guide for installing the Mojo Software Development Kit (SDK) on your system:

-**System Requirements:** Ensure your system meets the minimum requirements for running Mojo. In general, you'll need an x86-64 CPU with SSE4.2 instruction set, at least 8 GB of RAM, and Python 3.8 or later installed.

-**Download the Modular CLI:** Head over to the official Mojo website (https://www.modular.com/max/mojo) and download the Modular CLI installer for your operating system (Windows, macOS, or Linux).

-**Install the Modular CLI:** Run the downloaded installer and follow the on-screen instructions to complete the installation.

-**Install the Mojo SDK:** Open a terminal or command prompt window. Run the following command to install the Mojo SDK:

```
modular install mojo
```

Setting Up Environment Variables (Optional):

While not strictly necessary, setting up environment variables can improve your development workflow. Here's how to do it for commonly used shells (refer to your specific platform's documentation for detailed instructions):

Bash:
```
export MOJO_PATH=$(modular config mojo.path)
echo 'export PATH="$MOJO_PATH/bin:$PATH"' >> ~/.bashrc
source ~/.bashrc
```

ZSH:

```
export MOJO_PATH=$(modular config mojo.path)
echo 'export PATH="$MOJO_PATH/bin:$PATH"' >> ~/.zshrc
source ~/.zshrc
```

This sets the `MOJO_PATH` environment variable to point to the Mojo installation directory and adds the Mojo bin directory to your system's search path. This allows you to run Mojo commands directly from the terminal without specifying the full path.

Verifying the Installation:

Once the installation is complete, open a terminal and type:

```
mojo --version
```

This command should display the installed Mojo version, confirming successful installation.

Choosing Your Development Environment:

Now that you have Mojo installed, it's time to choose your development environment. If you're new to programming, consider starting with a simple text editor like Notepad++. As you progress, explore using an IDE like Visual Studio Code for a more feature-rich experience. Online playgrounds can be handy for quick experimentation without software installation.

The Next Steps:

With your development environment set up, you're ready to delve into the exciting world of Mojo programming. The next chapter will guide you through writing your first Mojo program and introduce the basic building blocks of the Mojo language.

2.2 Grasping the Mojo Syntax - Building Blocks for Automation

Having set up your development environment, it's time to dive into the core elements of Mojo syntax. This chapter equips you with the foundational knowledge to construct your first Mojo programs. We'll explore variables, data types, operators, and keywords – the building blocks that bring your RPA solutions to life.

1. Variables and Data Types:

Variables: Variables act as containers that store data within your program. You can give them meaningful names to represent the data they hold.

Data Types: Data types define the kind of data a variable can store. Common data types in Mojo include:

-int: Integers (whole numbers)

-float: Decimal numbers

-bool: Boolean values (True or False)

-string: Text data

Declaring Variables:

Code snippet

```
# Declare an integer variable named 'age' and assign the value 30
var age: int = 30
```

```
# Declare a string variable named 'name' with
your name
var name: string = "Alice"

# Declare a boolean variable named 'is_active'
and set it to True
var is_active: bool = True
```

2. Operators:

Operators perform operations on data stored in variables or constants. Here are some common operators in Mojo:

-Arithmetic Operators: (+, -, *, /) for performing mathematical calculations.

-Comparison Operators: (==, !=, <, >, <=, >=) for comparing values.

-Logical Operators: (and, or, not) for combining conditions.

-Assignment Operator: (=) to assign values to variables.

Code Examples:

Code snippet

```
# Add two numbers and store the result in 'sum'
var num1: int = 10
var num2: int = 20
var sum: int = num1 + num2   # sum will be 30

# Check if a number is even
var number: int = 12
var is_even: bool = number % 2 == 0   # is_even
will be True (divisible by 2)
```

3. Keywords:

Keywords are reserved words with special meanings within the Mojo language. Here are some commonly used keywords:

- **var:** Used to declare variables.

- **if:** Used to create conditional statements.

- **else:** Used for alternative execution paths in conditional statements.

- **for:** Used to create loop statements for repetitive tasks.

- **while:** Used to create loops that continue as long as a condition is True.

- **print:** Used to output data to the console.

Code Example:

Code snippet

```
# Check if a user is eligible to vote (age >= 18)
var age: int = 25
if age >= 18:
  print("Eligible to vote")
else:
  print("Not eligible to vote")
```

4. Comments:

Comments are lines of text ignored by the compiler but provide explanations within your code. They enhance readability and make your code easier to understand for yourself and others.

Code snippet

```
// This is a single-line comment

/* This is a multi-line comment */
```

Summary:

By understanding these core elements – variables, data types, operators, keywords, and comments – you've laid the foundation for building powerful Mojo programs. The next chapters will explore these concepts further and introduce more advanced functionalities to equip you for crafting effective RPA solutions.

2.3 Mastery over Data: Variables and Data Types in Mojo

1. Unveiling the Data Type Arsenal:

Mojo supports a variety of data types to represent different kinds of information your program works with. Here are some of the most commonly used ones:

-Integers (int): Whole numbers (e.g., 10, -5, 300). Integers are ideal for storing quantities, counts, or any data that doesn't involve decimals.

-Floats (float): Decimal numbers (e.g., 3.14, -12.56, 99.99). Floats are used for calculations involving decimals or representing continuous values.

-Booleans (bool): Logical values representing True or False. Booleans are crucial for making decisions and controlling program flow based on conditions.

-Strings (string): Sequences of characters representing text data (e.g., "Hello World!", "Alice Smith", "Product ID: 123"). Strings are used to store names, descriptions, and any textual information.

2. Declaring and Initializing Variables:

In Mojo, you declare variables using the `var` keyword followed by the variable name and a colon (:). You can optionally specify the data type to ensure type safety and improve code readability. Here's how to declare and initialize variables with different data types:

Code snippet

```
# Declare an integer variable named 'age' and assign the value 25
var age: int = 25

# Declare a float variable named 'pi' with the value of pi
var pi: float = 3.14159

# Declare a boolean variable named 'is_registered' and set it to True
var is_registered: bool = True

# Declare a string variable named 'name' to store your full name
var name: string = "John Doe"
```

3. Using Variables Effectively:

Once declared, you can use variable names to access and manipulate the stored data. Here are some examples:

Performing Calculations:

Code snippet

```
# Calculate the area of a rectangle (length *
width)
var length: int = 10
var width: int = 5
var area: int = length * width
print("Area of rectangle:", area)
```

String Manipulation:

Code snippet

```
# Greet the user by name
var name: string = "Alice"
var greeting: string = "Hello, " + name + "!"
print(greeting)
```

Conditional Statements:

Code snippet

```
# Check if a number is positive
var number: int = -7
if number > 0:
  print("The number is positive")
else:
  print("The number is non-positive")
```

4. Implicit Data Type Conversion:

In some cases, Mojo can perform implicit data type conversion. For example, you can assign an integer value to a float variable.

However, it's generally recommended to be explicit with data types to avoid potential errors and improve code clarity.

5. Exploring Additional Data Types:

Mojo offers additional data types for more complex data structures:

-Lists: Ordered collections of items, similar to arrays in other languages.

-Maps: Key-value pairs for storing data like dictionaries in other languages.

We'll explore these advanced data types in later chapters as we delve into more intricate functionalities of Mojo programming for RPA development.

By mastering variables and data types, you've unlocked the power to store, manage, and manipulate data effectively within your Mojo programs. This paves the way for building robust and versatile RPA solutions.

2.4 Your First Steps in Mojo Programming - Building a Simple Program

Congratulations! You've grasped the fundamentals of Mojo syntax and data types. Now, let's put your knowledge into action by crafting your first Mojo program. In this chapter, we'll guide you through building a simple program to greet a user by name.

1. Program Objective:

Our program will prompt the user for their name, store it in a variable, and then display a personalized greeting message.

2. Coding the Program:

Open your preferred Mojo development environment (IDE or text editor) and create a new file. Here's the Mojo code for the program:

Code snippet

```
// Get user's name
print("Enter your name: ")
var name: string = readln()   // Read user input and store in 'name' variable

// Construct the greeting message
var greeting: string = "Hello, " + name + "!"

// Display the greeting message
print(greeting)
```

Explanation:

Line 1: This line adds a comment explaining the purpose of the initial code block (getting the user's name).

Line 2: We use the `print` function to display a message prompting the user to enter their name.

Line 3: The `readln` function reads the user's input from the console and stores it in the `name` variable, which is declared as a string type.

Line 5: We create a new string variable named `greeting`. The `+` operator is used to concatenate the strings "Hello, ", the value stored in the `name` variable, and an exclamation mark.

Line 7: Finally, we use `print` again to display the constructed greeting message.

3. Running the Program:

Saving the Program: Save the code you wrote in a file with a `.mojo` extension (e.g., `first_program.mojo`).

Running from the Terminal: Open a terminal or command prompt window and navigate to the directory where you saved your program.

Mojo Command: Use the `mojo run` command followed by the filename to execute your program. Here's an example:

```
mojo run first_program.mojo
```

4. Testing and Experimentation:

Run the Program: Execute the `mojo run` command as explained above. The program should prompt you to enter your name.

Enter Your Name: Type your name in the terminal and press Enter.

Output: The program should display a personalized greeting message like "Hello, Alice!" (replacing Alice with your actual name).

5. Experimentation:

Feel free to modify the program and experiment:

-Change the greeting message to something more creative.

-Try adding another prompt to ask for the user's age and display a different message based on the age.

By building and running this simple program, you've successfully taken your first steps into the exciting world of Mojo programming. As you progress through the following chapters, you'll explore more advanced concepts and functionalities to craft powerful RPA solutions for automating repetitive tasks.

Chapter 3: Mastering Mojo Control Flow

3.1 Taking Control with Conditionals: if/else in Mojo

In the previous chapters, you explored variables, data types, and basic program structures. Now, we delve into the realm of conditional statements, specifically the `if` and `else` statements. These statements empower your Mojo programs to make decisions and execute different code blocks based on specific conditions.

1. The Power of Conditionals:

Conditional statements are fundamental building blocks in any programming language. They allow your program to evaluate conditions and execute different sets of instructions based on whether the condition is True or False. This adds flexibility and decision-making capabilities to your programs.

2. The `if` Statement:

The `if` statement forms the core of conditional logic. It takes a condition as an argument. If the condition evaluates to True, the code block indented within the `if` statement is executed.

Syntax:

Code snippet

```
if (condition):
```

```
# Code to execute if the condition is True
```

Example:

Code snippet

```
var age: int = 20

if age >= 18:
  print("You are eligible to vote")
```

In this example, the program checks if the value in the `age` variable is greater than or equal to 18. If the condition is True (age is 20 or above), the message "You are eligible to vote" is printed.

3. **The `else` Statement:**

The `else` statement provides an alternative path for program execution. It's used in conjunction with the `if` statement and defines the code block to execute if the condition in the `if` statement is False.

Syntax:

Code snippet

```
if (condition):
  # Code to execute if the condition is True
else:
  # Code to execute if the condition is False
```

Example:

Code snippet

```
var grade: string = "B"

if grade == "A":
  print("Excellent work!")
else:
  print("Keep practicing, you can improve!")
```

Here, the program checks if the value in the `grade` variable is "A". If it's not "A" (i.e., the condition is False), the `else` block executes, and the message "Keep practicing..." is printed.

4. Nested `if` Statements:

You can create more complex decision-making logic by nesting `if` statements within each other. An inner `if` statement can be placed within the code block of an outer `if` or `else` statement.

Example:

Code snippet

```
var day: string = "Saturday"

if day == "Saturday":
  print("It's the weekend!")
   if day == "Saturday" and time >= 12:  # Nested if within Saturday block
     print("Enjoy your afternoon!")
else:
  print("Have a productive week!")
```

In this example, the outer `if` statement checks if the day is "Saturday". If it is, the inner `if` statement (nested within the `Saturday` block) checks if it's also past noon. This combination of conditions allows for more granular control over program flow.

5. Conclusion:

By mastering `if` and `else` statements, you equip your Mojo programs with the ability to make decisions and execute code selectively based on various conditions. This is essential for building robust and adaptable RPA solutions that can handle different scenarios within a workflow. The next chapter will explore another type of conditional statement - the `while` loop - for repetitive tasks.

3.2 Conquering Repetition with Loops: for and while in Mojo

In the previous chapter, you explored conditional statements to control program flow based on specific conditions. Now, we delve into the world of loops - powerful tools for automating repetitive tasks within your Mojo programs. This chapter introduces two common loop constructs in Mojo: `for` loops and `while` loops.

1. Understanding Loops:

Loops allow you to execute a block of code repeatedly until a certain condition is met. This is particularly useful for automating tasks that involve processing sequences of data or performing actions multiple times.

2. The `for` Loop:

The `for` loop is ideal for iterating over a predefined sequence of elements, typically a collection of items stored in a list. It executes a code block for each item in the sequence.

Syntax:

Code snippet

```
for item in sequence:
  # Code to execute for each item in the sequence
```

Example:

Code snippet

```
# Sample list of fruits
var fruits: list[string] = ["apple", "banana", "orange", "mango"]

for fruit in fruits:
  print("I like to eat", fruit)
```

In this example, the `for` loop iterates over each item (fruit name) in the `fruits` list. For each iteration, the variable `fruit` takes on the value of the current item, and the message "I like to eat" is printed along with the fruit name.

3. The `while` Loop:

The `while` loop offers more flexibility for repetitive tasks where the number of iterations might not be predetermined. It continues executing a code block as long as a specified condition remains True.

Syntax:

Code snippet

```
while (condition):
    # Code to execute as long as the condition is True
```

Example:

Code snippet

```
# Guessing game (simple example)
var secret_number: int = 7
var guess: int

while guess != secret_number:
   guess = readln("Guess a number between 1 and 10: ")
   guess = int(guess)   # Convert string input to integer

if guess == secret_number:
     print("Congratulations, you guessed the number!")
```

Here, the `while` loop keeps prompting the user for guesses until the guessed number (`guess`) matches the secret number (`secret_number`). The loop continues iterating as long as the condition (`guess != secret_number`) is True.

4. Breaking Out of Loops (Optional):

Mojo provides the `break` keyword that allows you to exit a loop prematurely if a specific condition is met within the loop.

5. Choosing the Right Loop:

-Use `for` loops when you know the exact number of iterations needed or when you're working with a predefined sequence of data.

-Use `while` loops when the number of iterations depends on a condition that needs to be evaluated repeatedly.

6. Summary:

By mastering loops, you can automate repetitive tasks efficiently within your Mojo programs. `for` loops excel at iterating over known sequences, while `while` loops provide flexibility for handling conditions that determine the number of iterations. These functionalities are essential for building robust RPA solutions that can process data sets, interact with applications repeatedly, and streamline workflows. The next chapter will introduce functions - reusable blocks of code - to further enhance your Mojo programming capabilities.

3.3 Safeguarding Your Programs: Error Handling in Mojo

Even the most meticulously crafted Mojo programs can encounter errors during execution. These errors can arise from various sources, including invalid user input, unexpected data formats, or network issues. This chapter equips you with techniques for handling errors gracefully, preventing program crashes, and ensuring the robustness of your RPA solutions.

1. Potential Errors in Mojo Programs:

Here are some common errors you might encounter in Mojo:

Runtime Errors: These occur during program execution due to issues like division by zero, accessing non-existent variables, or attempting invalid operations.

Input Errors: These arise from unexpected user input that doesn't conform to program expectations (e.g., entering a string when a number is required).

File I/O Errors: Errors can occur while reading from or writing to files due to missing files, insufficient permissions, or disk errors.

Network Errors: Network-related tasks might fail due to connectivity issues, server unavailability, or timeouts.

2. The Importance of Error Handling:

Unhandled errors can lead to program crashes, unexpected behavior, and disruptions in your RPA workflows. Implementing proper error handling mechanisms allows you to:

Catch errors: Identify and isolate errors when they occur.

Provide informative messages: Display user-friendly error messages explaining the issue encountered.

Take corrective actions: Recover from errors gracefully, potentially offering retry options or logging error details for troubleshooting.

Maintain program stability: Prevent program crashes and ensure the overall robustness of your RPA solutions.

3. The `try/except` Block:

Mojo offers the `try/except` block as a fundamental tool for error handling. The `try` block contains the code that might potentially encounter errors. The `except` block defines how to handle errors if they occur within the `try` block.

Syntax:

Code snippet

```
try:
```

```
    # Code that might raise errors
except (ExceptionType):    # Optional: Specify the type of error to handle
    # Code to execute if an error occurs
```

Example (Handling division by zero):

Code snippet

```
var denominator: int = 0

try:
    result = 10 / denominator   # Potential division by zero error
    print("Result:", result)
except (ZeroDivisionError):
    print("Error: Cannot divide by zero")
```

In this example, the `try` block attempts to divide 10 by the value in `denominator` (which is 0). This would cause a division by zero error. The `except` block catches this specific error (`ZeroDivisionError`) and prints an error message instead of crashing the program.

4. Additional Considerations:

-**Multiple `except` Blocks:** You can have multiple `except` blocks to handle different types of errors more specifically.

-**`else` Block:** Optionally, you can include an `else` block after the `except` blocks. The `else` block executes only if no errors occur within the `try` block.

5. Conclusion:

By incorporating error handling mechanisms using `try/except` blocks, you build resilience into your Mojo programs. This ensures they can gracefully handle unexpected situations, improving the reliability and user experience of your RPA solutions. The following chapter delves into functions - reusable building blocks of code - to enhance code organization and maintainability.

3.4 Unveiling the Mystery: Debugging Your Mojo Programs

So far, you've conquered the fundamentals of Mojo programming and built your initial RPA skillset. However, even the most seasoned programmers encounter errors and unexpected behavior in their code. This chapter equips you with debugging strategies to identify, understand, and fix issues within your Mojo programs.

1. Recognizing the Need to Debug:

There are telltale signs that your Mojo program might have errors:

-Errors During Execution: The program crashes or displays error messages.

-Unexpected Output: The program produces incorrect results or behaves differently than expected.

-Logic Errors: The program seems to run but doesn't achieve the desired outcome due to flaws in the program logic.

2. Debugging Strategies:

Here's a systematic approach to debugging your Mojo programs:

-Pinpoint the Error: Reproduce the issue consistently and identify the specific line of code or code block causing the problem.

- **Analyze Error Messages:** Pay close attention to error messages displayed by the program. They often provide valuable clues about the nature of the error.

- **Print Statements:** Insert `print` statements at strategic points in your code to inspect the values of variables during program execution. This can help you trace the flow of data and identify where things go wrong.

- **Logical Code Review:** Carefully review your code line by line, paying attention to syntax errors, typos, and potential logical flaws in the implemented algorithms.

- **Test Incrementally:** Break down your program into smaller, testable chunks. Test each section individually to isolate the problematic part of the code.

3. Debugging Tools (if applicable):

Some Mojo development environments (IDEs) offer debugging tools that can significantly aid in the debugging process. These tools might provide features like:

- **Setting Breakpoints:** Pause program execution at specific lines of code to examine variable values and step through the code line by line.

- **Call Stack Inspection:** View the sequence of function calls that led to the current point in the program, helping you identify where an error originated.

- **Variable Inspection:** Examine the values of variables at any point during program execution.

4. Tips for Effective Debugging:

- **Start Simple:** Begin by isolating the problematic section of code. Fix one issue at a time.

-**Methodical Approach:** Don't make random changes to your code. Follow a systematic debugging strategy.

-**Document Your Steps:** Keep track of the debugging process, the changes you make, and the observed results. This can help you backtrack if needed.

-**Use Online Resources:** Search for solutions or error messages online. The Mojo community forums and documentation might offer valuable insights.

5. Conclusion:

Debugging is an essential skill for any programmer. By mastering these debugging techniques and using available tools effectively, you'll be well-equipped to identify, fix, and prevent errors in your Mojo programs. This ensures your RPA solutions function as intended, leading to robust and reliable automations. The final chapter will explore more advanced Mojo functionalities to empower you to create even more versatile RPA solutions.

Chapter 4: Working with Data in Mojo

4.1 Taming the Data: Manipulation Techniques in Mojo

Throughout your Mojo programming journey, you'll interact with various data types. This chapter delves into methods for manipulating strings, dates, times, and numbers – essential techniques for building robust RPA solutions.

1. String Manipulation Magic:

Strings are sequences of characters used to represent text data. Mojo offers a variety of methods for processing and modifying strings:

Slicing: Extract substrings from a string using start and end indexes within square brackets.

Code snippet

```
name: string = "Alice Smith"
first_name = name[0:5]  # Extract characters from index 0 to 4 (excluding index 5)
print("First name:", first_name)  # Output: Alice
```

Concatenation: Combine strings using the + operator to create new strings.

Code snippet

```
greeting = "Hello, " + name
```

41

```
print(greeting)    # Output: Hello, Alice Smith
```

Finding Substrings: Use the `find` method to locate the starting index of a substring within a string.

Code snippet

```
full_name = "Alice Smith"
index = full_name.find("Smith")
if index != -1:
  print("Last name found at index:", index)
else:
  print("Last name not found")
```

Replacing Substrings: The `replace` method allows you to replace occurrences of a substring with another substring.

Code snippet

```
old_text = "This is an example text"
new_text = old_text.replace("example", "replaced")
print(new_text)    # Output: This is a replaced text
```

Converting Case: Use the `upper` and `lower` methods to convert strings to uppercase or lowercase, respectively.

Code snippet

```
message = "MiXeD CaSe TeXt"
uppercase_message = message.upper()
```

```
lowercase_message = message.lower()
print(uppercase_message)    # Output: MIXED CASE TEXT
print(lowercase_message)    # Output: mixed case text
```

2. Working with Dates and Times:

The `date` **and** `time` **Modules:** Mojo provides the `date` and `time` modules for working with dates and times. These modules offer functions for creating date and time objects, formatting dates/times, and performing date/time calculations.

Code snippet

```
from date import today   # Import today function from date module

current_date = today()
formatted_date = current_date.format("YYYY-MM-DD")   # Format date as yyyy-mm-dd
print("Today's date:", formatted_date)
```

Date/Time Arithmetic: You can perform basic arithmetic operations on date and time objects to add or subtract days, hours, minutes, etc.

Code snippet

```
from date import timedelta

# Add 7 days to the current date
future_date = today() + timedelta(days=7)
```

```
print("Date              after           7           days:",
future_date.format("DD-MMM-YYYY"))
```

3. Number Manipulation:

-Basic Arithmetic Operators: Mojo supports basic arithmetic operators (+, -, *, /) for performing calculations on numerical data.

-Mathematical Functions: The `math` module offers various mathematical functions like `sqrt` for square root, `ceil` for ceiling, and `floor` for floor.

Code snippet

```
from math import sqrt

number = 16
square_root = sqrt(number)
print("Square root of 16:", square_root)
```

Type Conversion: You can use the `int`, `float`, and `str` functions to convert between number data types (e.g., converting a string representation of a number to an integer).

Code snippet

```
user_input = readln("Enter a number: ")
number = int(user_input)   # Convert string input to integer
calculation = number * 5
print("Result:", calculation)
```

4. Summary:

By mastering these data manipulation techniques, you'll be able to effectively process and transform various data types within your Mojo programs. This empowers you to build RPA solutions that can handle complex data parsing, formatting, and calculations, creating a solid foundation for automating tasks that involve text processing, date/time manipulations, and numerical computations. As you progress in your RPA development journey, you'll explore more advanced functionalities in Mojo to tackle even more intricate automation challenges.

4.2 Conquering Data Sources: Extracting and Handling Information

In the previous chapters, you explored core functionalities and data manipulation techniques in Mojo. Now, we delve into how to interact with various data sources that are fundamental for most RPA workflows. You'll learn how to extract, parse, and transform data from spreadsheets, databases, and text files.

1. Accessing Spreadsheets:

-The `openpyxl` **Module:** For working with Excel spreadsheets (.xlsx files), Mojo leverages the `openpyxl` module. You can use this module to read data from cells, manipulate worksheets, and even write data back to spreadsheets.

Code snippet

```
from openpyxl import load_workbook

# Open a spreadsheet
workbook = load_workbook("data.xlsx")
sheet = workbook["Sheet1"]   # Access a specific sheet
```

```
# Read data from a cell
cell_value = sheet["A1"].value
print("Value in cell A1:", cell_value)
```

2. Interacting with Databases:

Database Connectivity Libraries: Mojo can interact with various databases using external libraries specific to the database technology (e.g., `pyodbc` for connecting to MS SQL Server, `psycopg2` for PostgreSQL). You'll need to install these libraries separately.

Code snippet

```
# Example using pymysql for MySQL (assuming it's installed)
import pymysql

# Connect to MySQL database
connection = pymysql.connect(host="localhost", user="username", password="password", database="mydatabase")
cursor = connection.cursor()

# Execute a query and fetch results
cursor.execute("SELECT * FROM customers")
results = cursor.fetchall()

# Process the results (e.g., loop through each row)
for row in results:
    print(row[0], row[1])   # Assuming row[0] is customer ID and row[1] is name
```

```
# Close the connection
connection.close()
```

3. Reading Text Files:

The `open` **Function:** The built-in `open` function in Mojo allows you to read data from text files. You can specify the reading mode ("r" for reading) and iterate through lines of text in the file.

Code snippet

```
# Open a text file for reading
file = open("data.txt", "r")

# Read lines from the file
lines = file.readlines()

# Process each line (e.g., extract data or perform string manipulation)
for line in lines:
    print(line.strip())   # Remove trailing newline character using strip()

# Close the file
file.close()
```

4. Data Parsing and Transformation:

Once you extract data from these sources, you'll often need to parse and transform it into a format suitable for further processing within your RPA solution. Mojo's string manipulation techniques (covered in Chapter 10) and conditional statements (Chapter 6) come into play for this purpose.

-**Extracting Specific Data:** You can use string slicing, regular expressions (advanced topic), or other techniques to extract specific parts of the data from each line or cell value.

-**Data Cleaning:** You might need to handle missing values, remove unwanted characters, or convert data types (e.g., strings to numbers) to ensure clean and consistent data for further processing.

5. Summary:

By mastering techniques for data extraction and manipulation from various sources, you empower your Mojo programs to interact with the real world. This allows you to automate tasks that involve gathering data from spreadsheets, databases, or text files, transforming it as needed, and using the extracted information to perform further actions within your RPA workflows. The following chapter explores functions - reusable building blocks of code - to further enhance your Mojo programming capabilities.

4.3 Shaping the Data: Formatting and Transformation for Automation

In the previous chapter, you explored how to extract data from various sources. Now, we delve into techniques for formatting and transforming that data to meet the specific requirements within your Mojo automation processes.

1. The Power of Formatting:

Data extracted from various sources might not always be in the perfect format for your automation needs. Formatting techniques ensure the data is presented in a consistent and usable manner for your Mojo programs.

String Formatting: The `format` method (similar to Python's f-strings) allows you to insert variables or expressions within strings to create formatted output.

Code snippet

```
name: string = "Alice"
age: int = 30

greeting = "Hello, {}! You are {} years old.".format(name, age)
print(greeting)   # Output: Hello, Alice! You are 30 years old.
```

Date and Time Formatting: The `date` and `time` modules (introduced in Chapter 10) offer various methods to format dates and times according to specific patterns (e.g., "YYYY-MM-DD" or "DD/MM/YYYY").

Code snippet

```
from date import today

current_date = today()
formatted_date = current_date.format("%B %d, %Y")
# Format as "Month Day, Year"
print("Today's date:", formatted_date)
```

Number Formatting: You can use string formatting techniques or functions like `str` to convert numbers to strings and control the number of decimal places displayed.

Code snippet

```
price = 123.4567
formatted_price = "{:.2f}".format(price)   # Limit to 2 decimal places
print("Price:", formatted_price)      # Output: Price: 123.46
```

2. Data Conversion Techniques:

In some cases, you might need to convert data between different data types to ensure compatibility within your program logic.

Built-in Functions: Mojo provides functions like `int`, `float`, and `str` to convert between integers, floats, and strings.

Code snippet

```
user_input = readln("Enter a number: ")
number = float(user_input)   # Convert string input to float

# Check if the number is an integer (without decimals)
if number.is_integer():
  print("The number is an integer")
else:
  print("The number is a decimal")
```

String Parsing: When working with text data, you might need to parse strings to extract numerical values or convert them to specific formats. String manipulation techniques (Chapter 10) can be helpful for this purpose.

3. Conditional Formatting:

You can leverage conditional statements (Chapter 6) to format data based on specific conditions.

Code snippet

```
grade: string = "B"

if grade == "A":
  formatted_grade = "Excellent!"
elif grade == "B":
  formatted_grade = "Good work"
else:
  formatted_grade = "Keep practicing"

print("Your grade:", formatted_grade)
```

4. Summary:

By mastering data formatting and transformation techniques, you ensure the data extracted from various sources aligns with the requirements of your Mojo programs. This allows for seamless processing, manipulation, and utilization of data within your RPA workflows. As you progress in your RPA development journey, you'll explore more advanced functionalities in Mojo to tackle even more intricate automation challenges.

4.4 Safeguarding Your Data: Validation Techniques in Mojo

Data validation is a crucial aspect of ensuring data integrity within your Mojo automation processes. This chapter delves into techniques for implementing data validation checks in your Mojo programs to identify and handle invalid or unexpected data.

1. The Importance of Data Validation:

Data extracted from various sources or user input might contain errors or inconsistencies. Validation checks act as a safety net, preventing invalid data from entering your automation workflows. This helps to:

Improve Data Quality: By ensuring data conforms to expected formats and ranges, you minimize errors in downstream processing steps.

Prevent Errors: Validation helps to catch invalid data early on, preventing program crashes and unexpected behavior.

Enhance User Experience: Providing clear error messages when invalid data is entered allows users to correct their input and ensures a smoother automation experience.

2. Common Data Validation Techniques:

Here are some common data validation techniques you can implement in Mojo:

Data Type Checks: Ensure data is of the expected type (e.g., checking if user input is a number when a numerical value is required).

Code snippet

```
user_input = readln("Enter your age: ")

try:
   age = int(user_input)   # Attempt to convert input to integer
  if age < 0:
    raise ValueError("Age cannot be negative")
  # Proceed with valid age
except ValueError:
```

```
    print("Error: Invalid age entered. Please enter
a non-negative number.")
```

-Range Checks: Validate if numerical data falls within a specific range (e.g., ensuring a product ID is within a valid range).

-Pattern Matching: Use regular expressions (advanced topic) to check if data adheres to a specific pattern (e.g., validating email addresses).

-Required Field Checks: Ensure mandatory fields are not left empty by users.

3. Leveraging `if` Statements and Error Handling:

The `if` statement (Chapter 6) forms the foundation for implementing validation checks. You can create conditions to test if data meets your validation criteria. The `try/except` block (Chapter 8) is essential for handling errors gracefully when validation fails.

4. Additional Considerations:

-User-Friendly Error Messages: Provide informative error messages that clearly explain the validation issue encountered. This helps users understand how to correct their input.

-Custom Validation Functions: As your automation needs become more complex, consider creating reusable functions for specific validation tasks, promoting code modularity and maintainability.

5. Summary:

By incorporating data validation techniques within your Mojo programs, you safeguard the integrity of your data and ensure the smooth operation of your RPA workflows. This not only improves the robustness of your automations but also enhances the user experience by preventing errors and providing clear guidance when invalid data is encountered. As you progress in your RPA development journey, you'll explore more advanced functionalities in Mojo to tackle even more intricate automation challenges.

Chapter 5: Mojo for User Interface (UI) Automation

5.1 Mastering the GUI: Automating Desktop Applications with Mojo

In previous chapters, you've conquered essential Mojo programming concepts and data manipulation techniques. Now, we delve into a powerful aspect of RPA: interacting with desktop applications using Mojo. This chapter equips you with the tools to automate tasks that involve interacting with elements like buttons, text fields, and menus within graphical user interfaces (GUIs) of desktop applications.

1. The Power of GUI Automation:

Imagine automating repetitive tasks within applications you use daily. Mojo empowers you to achieve this by simulating user interactions like clicks, typing, and selections. This can streamline workflows, save time, and minimize errors in manual processes.

2. Leveraging the `robot` Module:

Mojo's `robot` module provides functionalities for interacting with GUI elements. Here's an overview of key methods:

-`robot.mouse_move(x, y)`: Moves the mouse pointer to a specific screen coordinate (x, y).

-`robot.click()`: Simulates a left mouse button click at the current mouse position.

-`robot.type(text)`: Types the specified text into the active window.

`-robot.press(key)`: Presses a specific keyboard key.

`-robot.release(key)`: Releases a previously pressed keyboard key.

3. Identifying UI Elements:

To interact with elements effectively, you'll need to identify them within the application's GUI. Here are common approaches:

-Manual Observation: Carefully examine the application's interface to locate the elements you want to interact with (buttons, text fields, etc.).

-UI Inspection Tools (Optional): Some advanced development tools can help inspect desktop application UIs and provide details about elements, which can aid in identification.

4. Building Automation Scripts:

Here's a basic example demonstrating how to automate a simple login process in a desktop application:

Code snippet

```
from robot import robot

# Move mouse to the username field (replace coordinates as needed)
robot.mouse_move(100, 150)
robot.click()

# Type the username
robot.type("your_username")

# Move mouse to the password field
robot.mouse_move(100, 200)
robot.click()
```

```
# Type the password (consider security measures
when storing passwords in code)
robot.type("your_password")

# Move mouse to the login button
robot.mouse_move(200, 250)
robot.click()

print("Login automation completed (replace
coordinates with actual values)")
```

5. Error Handling and Robustness:

-Dynamic Screen Elements: Desktop application layouts might vary depending on factors like screen resolution or scaling. Consider using relative positioning or UI element search techniques to make your scripts more adaptable.

-Error Handling: Implement error handling mechanisms (Chapter 8) to gracefully handle scenarios where elements might not be found or actions fail. This ensures the robustness of your automation scripts.

6. Additional Considerations:

-Security: Be cautious when automating tasks that involve entering sensitive information like passwords. Consider alternative authentication methods or encrypted storage if necessary.

-Application Updates: Desktop application updates can sometimes cause automation scripts to break due to UI changes. Be prepared to maintain your scripts as applications evolve.

7. Summary:

By mastering GUI automation techniques with Mojo, you unlock a new level of automation capabilities. You can streamline workflows that involve interacting with desktop applications, saving time and effort while reducing errors in repetitive tasks. Remember to prioritize error handling, security, and script maintainability for robust and reliable automation solutions. As you progress in your RPA development journey, you'll explore more advanced functionalities in Mojo to tackle even more intricate automation challenges.

5.2 Conquering the Web: Automating Browser Interactions with Mojo

In previous chapters, you've mastered core Mojo functionalities and explored techniques for interacting with desktop applications. Now, we delve into the realm of web automation - a cornerstone of RPA. This chapter equips you with the tools to automate tasks within web browsers, such as navigating web pages, filling out forms, and extracting data from websites.

1. The Power of Web Automation:

Web automation streamlines repetitive tasks performed in web browsers, saving time and effort. Imagine automating tasks like:

-Logging in to websites and filling out forms.

-Extracting data from web pages (prices, product information, etc.).

-Submitting forms and uploading files.

-Performing repetitive web searches and data scraping (with respect to website terms of service).

2. Leveraging the `browser` Module:

Mojo's `browser` module empowers you to interact with web pages programmatically. Here's an overview of key methods:

- `browser.open(url)`: Opens the specified URL in a new browser window.

- `browser.go_to(url)`: Navigates the current browser window to the specified URL.

- `browser.find_element(selector)`: Locates a web element on the page using a CSS selector or other search methods.

- `element.click()`: Simulates a click on the found web element.

- `element.type(text)`: Types the specified text into a form field or other input element.

- `browser.get_text(selector)`: Retrieves the text content of an element identified by a selector.

3. Web Element Identification:

To interact with specific elements on a web page, you need to identify them uniquely. Common methods include:

-CSS Selectors: This is the most common and versatile approach for identifying web elements using CSS selectors. You can target elements by their ID, class name, tag name, attributes, or a combination of these.

-XPath: XPath provides another way to locate elements based on their position within the HTML document structure.

4. Building Web Automation Scripts:

Here's a basic example demonstrating how to automate a login process on a website:

Code snippet

```
from browser import browser
```

```
# Open the website
browser.open("https://www.example.com/login")

# Find the username field and type the username
username_field = browser.find_element("input[name='username']")
username_field.type("your_username")

# Find the password field and type the password
# (consider security measures)
password_field = browser.find_element("input[name='password']")
password_field.type("your_password")

# Find the login button and click it
login_button = browser.find_element("button[type='submit']")
login_button.click()

print("Login automation completed (replace selectors with actual values)")
```

5. Filling Forms and Extracting Data:

Once you can identify form fields and elements, you can use the `element.type` method to fill them with data. To extract data from websites, use the `browser.get_text` method or similar techniques to retrieve the content of specific elements.

6. Error Handling and Robustness:

-Dynamic Web Pages: Websites can change their structure dynamically based on user interaction or external factors. Consider using relative selectors or waiting mechanisms (e.g., waiting for elements to load) to make your scripts more adaptable.

-Error Handling: Implement error handling mechanisms (Chapter 8) to gracefully handle scenarios where elements might not be found or actions fail. This ensures the robustness of your automation scripts.

7. Security and Legal Considerations:

-Security: Exercise caution when automating tasks that involve entering sensitive information like passwords. Consider alternative authentication methods or encrypted storage if necessary.

-Website Terms of Service: Be mindful of the website's terms of service when automating tasks. Avoid scraping data or performing actions that might violate their policies.

8. Summary:

By mastering web automation techniques with Mojo, you unlock a vast potential for automating web-based tasks, streamlining processes, and boosting productivity. Remember to prioritize error handling, security, legal compliance, and script maintainability for robust and reliable automation solutions. As you progress in your RPA development journey, you'll explore more advanced functionalities in Mojo to tackle even more intricate automation challenges.

5.3 Crafting Enduring Automation: Best Practices for Robust UI Automation Scripts in Mojo

In the previous chapters, you explored techniques for interacting with desktop applications and web browsers using Mojo. Now, we delve into best practices for designing reliable and maintainable UI automation scripts – essential for building robust RPA solutions.

1. Prioritize Maintainability:

Modular Design: Break down complex automation tasks into smaller, reusable functions. This promotes code organization and simplifies maintenance.

Code snippet

```
def login(username, password):
    # Find username and password fields, type credentials, and click login button
    # ... (implementation details)

def fill_out_form(data):
    # Find and fill out form fields based on data dictionary
    # ... (implementation details)

# Main program flow
login("your_username", "your_password")
fill_out_form(user_data)
```

-**Meaningful Variable Names:** Use descriptive variable names that reflect their purpose. This enhances code readability and understanding.

-**Comments:** Add comments to explain the logic behind code sections, especially for complex parts. This aids future maintenance and collaboration.

2. Embrace Error Handling:

-`try/except` **Blocks:** Implement `try/except` blocks to gracefully handle exceptions that might occur during UI interactions. This prevents script crashes and allows for alternative actions or logging of errors.

Code snippet

```
from robot import robot

try:
  # UI interaction code (e.g., robot.click())
except Exception as e:
  print("Error:", e)
  # Handle the error (e.g., log the error, retry the action)
```

- **Specific Exception Handling:** Consider using specific exception types (e.g., `ElementNotFoundException`) to provide more targeted handling of different error scenarios.

3. Handle UI Changes with Flexibility:

- **Relative Selectors:** Whenever possible, favor relative selectors (e.g., using CSS sibling or parent-child relationships) over absolute selectors (based on specific coordinates) to make your scripts more adaptable to minor UI layout changes.

- **Wait Mechanisms:** Incorporate waiting mechanisms (e.g., using `time.sleep` with caution or waiting for elements to load) to account for potential delays in UI updates or element loading times.

4. Testing and Debugging:

- **Thorough Testing:** Test your automation scripts rigorously under various conditions (different screen resolutions, data inputs, etc.) to identify potential issues.

- **Debugging Techniques:** Leverage debugging tools (if available in your Mojo development environment) and logging techniques to pinpoint the root cause of errors during script execution.

5. Security Considerations:

-**Sensitive Information:** Be cautious when handling sensitive information like passwords. Consider alternative authentication methods (e.g., API tokens) or secure storage mechanisms if necessary.

-**Regular Updates:** As desktop applications and websites evolve, UI elements or structures might change. Be prepared to maintain your automation scripts to reflect these changes.

6. Summary:

By adhering to these best practices, you can design UI automation scripts in Mojo that are reliable, maintainable, and adaptable to changes. This ensures the long-term sustainability and effectiveness of your RPA solutions. As you progress in your RPA development journey, you'll explore more advanced functionalities in Mojo to tackle even more intricate automation challenges. Beyond the technical aspects, remember to consider the business context and user needs when designing your automation solutions. Aim for clear documentation, user-friendliness, and proper integration with existing workflows for successful RPA implementations.

Chapter 6: Leveraging Mojo for File and Folder Management

6.1 Taming the Filesystem: Automating File Operations with Mojo

In previous chapters, you explored techniques for interacting with various data sources and automating UI actions. Now, we delve into automating file system operations using Mojo, empowering you to manage files and folders programmatically within your RPA workflows.

1. The Power of File System Automation:

Imagine automating repetitive tasks like:

-Creating new files or folders based on specific criteria.

-Deleting temporary files or logs after processing.

-Renaming or moving files based on predefined rules.

By automating these tasks, you can streamline file management processes and improve the efficiency of your RPA solutions.

2. Leveraging the `os` Module:

Mojo utilizes the built-in `os` module to interact with the operating system's file system. Here's an overview of key methods for common file operations:

-`os.path.join(path1, path2, ...)`: Combines path components to create a valid file or folder path.

- `os.makedirs(path, exist_ok=True)`: Creates a directory (and any necessary parent directories) if it doesn't exist. The `exist_ok=True` argument prevents errors if the directory already exists.

- `open(filepath, mode='r')`: Opens a file for reading or writing (specify mode as 'r' for reading, 'w' for writing, or 'a' for appending).

- `file.write(data)`: Writes data to an opened file.

- `file.close()`: Closes an opened file handle.

- `os.remove(filepath)`: Deletes a file.

- `os.rename(old_path, new_path)`: Renames a file or folder.

- `shutil.move(source, destination)`: Moves a file or folder (consider using the `shutil` module for more advanced moving operations).

3. Code Examples for File Management Tasks:

Creating a New Text File:

Code snippet

```
import os

# Create a new text file named "data.txt"
filepath = os.path.join("C:/Users/your_username/Documents", "data.txt")  # Replace with your desired path
with open(filepath, "w") as file:
    file.write("This is some data written to the file.")

print("File created successfully!")
```

Deleting a File:

Code snippet

```
import os

# Delete a file named "temp.log"
filepath = os.path.join("C:/Temp", "temp.log")  # Replace with the path to your file
if os.path.exists(filepath):
    os.remove(filepath)
    print("File deleted successfully")
else:
    print("File not found")
```

Renaming a File:

Code snippet

```
import os

# Rename a file from "old_name.txt" to "new_name.txt"
old_filepath = os.path.join("C:/", "old_name.txt")  # Replace with your file paths
new_filepath = os.path.join("C:/", "new_name.txt")
os.rename(old_filepath, new_filepath)
print("File renamed successfully")
```

4. Additional Considerations:

-Error Handling: Implement error handling (Chapter 8) to gracefully handle potential issues like file not found exceptions or permission errors.

-Security: Be cautious when deleting or modifying files. Ensure your automation scripts have the necessary permissions and handle file operations securely.

-Path Management: Construct file paths carefully using `os.path.join` to ensure compatibility across different operating systems.

5. Summary:

By mastering file system automation techniques with Mojo, you can streamline file management tasks within your RPA solutions. This not only saves time but also reduces the risk of errors in manual file handling processes. Remember to prioritize error handling, security, and clear path construction for robust and reliable file management automation. As you progress in your RPA development journey, you'll explore more advanced functionalities in Mojo to tackle even more intricate automation challenges.

6.2 Conquering the Folderscape: Organizing and Managing Directories with Mojo

In the previous chapter, you explored automating basic file operations like creating, deleting, and renaming files. Now, we delve into techniques for managing folders (directories) using Mojo scripts. This empowers you to automate tasks like creating directory structures, deleting unnecessary folders, and iterating through files within folders for processing.

1. The Importance of Folder Management:

Effective folder management is crucial for maintaining a well-organized file system, especially when dealing with large volumes of data in RPA workflows. Automating folder operations can help you:

-Create Standardized Directory Structures: Ensure consistent folder hierarchies for easy file organization and retrieval.

-Automate Folder Cleanup: Schedule automatic deletion of temporary files or logs after processing.

-Iterate Through Files for Batch Processing: Process multiple files within a folder based on specific criteria.

2. Leveraging the `os` and `shutil` Modules:

We'll use a combination of the `os` module (introduced in Chapter 17) and the `shutil` module for more advanced folder management tasks:

-`os.makedirs(path, exist_ok=True)`: Creates a directory (and any necessary parent directories) if it doesn't exist.

-`os.listdir(path)`: Lists all files and folders within a directory.

-`os.path.isdir(path)`: Checks if a path points to a directory.

-`shutil.rmtree(path, ignore_errors=True)`: Removes a directory tree (including all files and subfolders) recursively. The `ignore_errors=True` argument prevents errors if the directory is empty or doesn't exist.

3. Creating Folder Structures:

Code snippet

```
import os

# Create a directory structure (e.g., /Documents/ProjectX/Data/Processed)
```

```python
base_path = os.path.join("C:/Users/your_username/Documents/ProjectX")
data_folder = os.path.join(base_path, "Data")
processed_folder = os.path.join(data_folder, "Processed")

os.makedirs(processed_folder, exist_ok=True)  # Create folders if they don't exist
print("Folder structure created successfully!")
```

4. Deleting Folders:

Code snippet

```python
import shutil

# Delete a folder named "temp" (be cautious with deletion)
folder_path = os.path.join("C:/Temp")
if os.path.isdir(folder_path):
  shutil.rmtree(folder_path, ignore_errors=True)
  print("Folder deleted successfully")
else:
  print("Folder not found")
```

5. Iterating Through Folders and Files:

Code snippet

```python
import os

# Process all .txt files within a directory
```

```
folder_path = "C:/Data"   # Replace with your folder path
for filename in os.listdir(folder_path):
    if filename.endswith(".txt"):   # Check file extension
        filepath = os.path.join(folder_path, filename)
        # Process the file here (e.g., open, read, modify)
        print("Processing file:", filename)
```

6. Additional Considerations:

-Error Handling: Implement error handling (Chapter 8) to gracefully handle exceptions like permission errors or issues during folder deletion.

-Security: Be cautious when deleting folders or modifying file structures. Ensure your automation scripts have the necessary permissions and handle operations securely.

-Nested Folder Structures: The `os.walk` function (not covered here but worth exploring) can be helpful for iterating through nested folder structures.

7. Summary:

By mastering folder management techniques with Mojo, you can automate tasks that keep your file system organized and streamline file processing within your RPA solutions. Remember to prioritize error handling, security, and clear path construction for robust and reliable folder management automation. As you progress in your RPA development journey, you'll explore more advanced functionalities in Mojo to tackle even more intricate automation challenges.

6.3 Embracing Diversity: Working with Various File Formats in Mojo

In previous chapters, you explored file system operations and folder management techniques. Now, we delve into working with different file formats, empowering you to extract and manipulate data from various sources like text files, CSV (Comma-Separated Values), and Excel spreadsheets within your Mojo automation programs.

1. The Challenge of File Formats:

RPA often involves processing data from diverse sources, each with its own file format. Mastering techniques for handling these formats expands the capabilities of your automation scripts.

2. Common File Formats:

-Text Files: Simple files containing plain text, often used for basic data storage and exchange.

-CSV Files: Comma-separated values files store data in a tabular format with rows and columns, suitable for structured data.

-Excel Spreadsheets: Powerful spreadsheets offering a grid-based layout for storing and manipulating data, often used for complex data analysis.

3. Techniques for Data Extraction and Manipulation:

Here's an overview of how to handle different file formats in Mojo:

Text Files:

`open(filepath, 'r')`: Open the file for reading.

`file.readlines()`: Read all lines of the file into a list.

String manipulation techniques (Chapter 10) Process the data line by line (e.g., split lines based on delimiters, extract specific information).

Code snippet

```
# Example: Reading data from a text file
with open("data.txt", "r") as file:
  lines = file.readlines()
  for line in lines:
    # Process each line of data
      print(line.strip())    # Remove trailing newline characters
```

CSV Files:

`csv` **module:** The `csv` module provides functionalities for reading and writing CSV files.

`csv.reader(file)`: Create a reader object to iterate through CSV rows.

Code snippet

```
import csv

# Example: Reading data from a CSV file
with open("data.csv", "r") as file:
  csv_reader = csv.reader(file)
  for row in csv_reader:
    # Access data in each row (cells)
      print(row[0], row[1])   # Assuming data is in columns 0 and 1
```

Excel Spreadsheets:

`openpyxl` **library (external):** Working with Excel spreadsheets in Mojo requires an external library like `openpyxl`. Installation instructions and usage details for external libraries might vary depending on your Mojo development environment.

`openpyxl` **methods:** The `openpyxl` library provides methods for reading and writing Excel data (cells, rows, columns, sheets).

Code snippet

```
# Example (using openpyxl, installation required):
from openpyxl import load_workbook

# Load the Excel workbook
workbook = load_workbook("data.xlsx")
sheet = workbook["Sheet1"]  # Assuming data is in the first sheet

# Access data from specific cells
cell_value = sheet["A1"].value  # Assuming data starts in cell A1

# Iterate through rows and columns
for row in sheet.iter_rows():
  for cell in row:
    print(cell.value)
```

4. Additional Considerations:

-File Format-Specific Libraries: Explore libraries or modules specifically designed for handling complex formats like Excel or image files (not covered here) for advanced manipulation capabilities.

-Error Handling: Implement error handling (Chapter 8) to gracefully handle issues like file corruption or unexpected data formats.

-Data Validation: Validate the extracted data to ensure it conforms to your expectations (e.g., data types, format).

5. Summary:

By mastering techniques for working with various file formats in Mojo, you unlock the potential to automate tasks that involve data extraction and manipulation from diverse sources. Remember to explore format-specific libraries, prioritize error handling, and validate extracted data for robust and reliable automation solutions. As you progress in your RPA development journey, you'll discover even more advanced functionalities in Mojo and external libraries to tackle intricate data processing challenges.

6.4 Uploading and Downloading with Ease: Automating File Transfers in Mojo

In previous chapters, you explored techniques for interacting with web pages and managing files on the local file system. Now, we delve into automating file uploads and downloads from web applications and servers, empowering your Mojo scripts to handle file transfer tasks seamlessly.

1. The Power of Automated File Transfers:

Imagine automating repetitive tasks like:

-Uploading product images to an e-commerce website.

-Downloading reports or logs from a server.

-Transferring files between different systems based on specific criteria.

By automating these tasks, you can save time and effort while ensuring consistency and efficiency in file transfer processes.

2. Techniques for Web Uploads and Downloads:

-Web Browser Interactions: Utilize Mojo's `browser` module (Chapter 15) to interact with web pages that involve file upload or download functionalities.

-Form Handling: Identify and interact with file input elements on web pages using CSS selectors or other methods.

`browser.send_keys(filepath)`: Simulate entering the path to the file you want to upload.

`browser.download_file(url, path=None)`: Download a file from a specified URL to a local directory (optional path argument to specify the download location).

Code snippet

```
from browser import browser

# Upload a file to a web application
browser.open("https://www.example.com/upload")
file_input                                       =
browser.find_element("input[type='file']")
file_input.send_keys("C:/path/to/your/file.txt")
# Replace with your file path
# Submit the upload form (implementation details
depend on the specific website)

# Download a file from a web server
```

```
download_url =
"https://www.example.com/report.pdf"
browser.download_file(download_url,
"C:/Downloads/report.pdf")    # Specify download
location
```

3. Uploading and Downloading from Servers:

File Transfer Protocol (FTP): Libraries like `ftplib` (built-in) or `paramiko` (external) can be used for programmatic file transfer via FTP (requires server credentials).

Secure File Transfer Protocol (SFTP): Similar to FTP, SFTP offers secure file transfer using `paramiko`.

Web APIs: If available, web APIs provided by the server can be used for programmatic file transfers (often requiring authentication tokens).

4. Secure Handling of File Paths and Credentials:

Environment Variables: Store sensitive information like file paths or server credentials in environment variables to avoid embedding them directly in your scripts.

Secret Management Tools: Consider using dedicated secret management tools for more secure storage and access control of sensitive data.

5. Additional Considerations:

Error Handling: Implement error handling (Chapter 8) to gracefully handle issues like file not found exceptions, connection errors, or invalid credentials.

Progress Tracking: For large file transfers, consider implementing mechanisms to track progress and provide user feedback.

Security Protocols: When using FTP or SFTP, ensure you're using secure connections (e.g., FTPS, SFTP) to protect data privacy during transfer.

6. Summary:

By mastering techniques for automating file uploads and downloads with Mojo, you can streamline file transfer processes within your RPA solutions. Remember to prioritize secure handling of file paths and credentials, implement error handling, and consider progress tracking for large transfers. As you progress in your RPA development journey, you'll explore advanced functionalities in Mojo and external libraries to tackle more intricate file transfer automation challenges.

Chapter 7: Integrating Mojo with Other Tools and Technologies

7.1 Bridging the Gap: Connecting Mojo to Databases and APIs

In previous chapters, you explored techniques for interacting with various data sources like files, web pages, and servers. Now, we delve into connecting Mojo programs to databases and APIs, significantly expanding the capabilities of your automation solutions.

1. The Power of Database and API Integration:

-Databases: Accessing and manipulating data stored in relational databases (e.g., MySQL, PostgreSQL) is crucial for many automation tasks.

-APIs (Application Programming Interfaces): Interacting with APIs allows you to leverage functionalities provided by external services or applications within your Mojo scripts.

2. Connecting to Databases:

The specific libraries or modules used for database connections in Mojo might vary depending on the database type. Here's a general approach:

-Import the Database Library: Import the appropriate library for your database (e.g., `pymysql` for MySQL, `psycopg2` for PostgreSQL).

- **Establish the Connection:** Create a connection object using the library's functions, providing necessary credentials (connection string, username, password).

- **Execute Queries:** Use the connection object to execute SQL queries to retrieve, insert, update, or delete data in the database.

- **Close the Connection:** Always close the database connection after you're done to release resources.

Code snippet

```
import pymysql  # Example using pymysql for MySQL

# Establish a connection
connection = pymysql.connect(host="localhost", user="your_username", password="your_password", database="your_database")
cursor = connection.cursor()

# Execute a query to retrieve data
cursor.execute("SELECT * FROM your_table")
data = cursor.fetchall()

# Process the retrieved data (e.g., print, store in variables)

# Close the connection
cursor.close()
connection.close()
```

3. Interacting with APIs:

requests **Library:** The requests library (often installed separately) is a popular choice for making HTTP requests to APIs in Mojo.

- **API Documentation:** Consult the API documentation for the specific API you want to interact with to understand its endpoints, authentication methods, and required parameters in the requests.

- **Sending Requests:** Use the `requests` library functions to send HTTP requests (GET, POST, PUT, DELETE) to API endpoints, providing necessary data in the request body or headers.

- **Handling Responses:** Parse the API response data (often in JSON or XML format) to extract relevant information for your automation purposes.

Code snippet

```python
import requests  # Example using requests library

# API endpoint URL and authentication details (replace with actual values)
api_url = "https://api.example.com/data"
api_key = "your_api_key"

# Send a GET request to the API
response = requests.get(api_url, headers={"Authorization": f"Bearer {api_key}"})

# Check for successful response
if response.status_code == 200:
    data = response.json()  # Assuming response is in JSON format
    # Process the retrieved data
else:
    print("Error:", response.status_code)
```

4. Additional Considerations:

- **Error Handling:** Implement error handling (Chapter 8) to gracefully handle connection errors, invalid credentials, or unexpected API responses.

- **Data Validation:** Validate the data retrieved from databases or APIs to ensure it conforms to your expectations.

- **Security:** Store database credentials and API keys securely using environment variables or secret management tools (Chapter 20).

5. Summary:

By mastering techniques for connecting Mojo to databases and APIs, you unlock a vast potential for data-driven automation. You can retrieve, manipulate, and integrate data from various sources, empowering your RPA solutions to handle complex tasks that extend beyond the limitations of standalone file operations and web interactions. Remember to prioritize secure handling of credentials, implement error handling, and validate data for robust and reliable automation solutions. As you progress in your RPA development journey, you'll explore advanced features in Mojo and external libraries to tackle even more intricate database and API integration challenges.

7.2 Expanding Horizons: Enhancing Mojo Programs with External Libraries

1. The Power of External Libraries:

- **Mojo Libraries:** Mojo offers a collection of built-in libraries providing functionalities for common tasks like interacting with the file system, web browsers, and databases.

- **External Libraries:** Beyond the built-in libraries, a vast ecosystem of external libraries exists, offering functionalities not natively included in Mojo.

2. When to Consider External Libraries:

-Specialized Tasks: If your automation script requires functionalities beyond Mojo's core capabilities, external libraries provide the necessary tools.

Examples: Working with advanced file formats (like Excel with `openpyxl`), interacting with specific APIs (using libraries like `googleapiclient`), or performing complex data analysis (with libraries like `pandas`).

-Community and Support: Many external libraries have active communities and extensive documentation, providing valuable resources for learning and troubleshooting.

3. Finding External Libraries:

Package Managers: Mojo's development environment might have a built-in package manager (consult your specific development environment documentation) to search for and install external libraries.

Online Repositories: Popular online repositories like PyPI (Python Package Index) host a vast collection of third-party libraries searchable by keyword or functionality.

4. Using External Libraries:

-Installation: Use the package manager or command-line tools (refer to your environment documentation) to install the desired library.

-Import the Library: Within your Mojo script, import the necessary modules from the installed library using the `import` statement.

-Utilize Library Functions: Access the functionalities offered by the library's modules and functions according to the library's documentation.

Code snippet

```python
# Example: Using the `openpyxl` library (assuming installed)
from openpyxl import load_workbook

# Load an Excel workbook
workbook = load_workbook("data.xlsx")
# Use library functions to access and manipulate data in the workbook
```

5. Important Considerations:

-Compatibility: Ensure the external library is compatible with your version of Mojo and the operating system you're working on.

-Documentation: Always refer to the library's documentation for detailed usage instructions, examples, and compatibility information.

-Security: Exercise caution when installing and using external libraries. Be sure to trust the source of the library and understand potential security implications.

6. Summary:

By leveraging external libraries, you can significantly enhance the capabilities of your Mojo programs. Explore the vast ecosystem of libraries available to address specific automation needs and expand the reach of your RPA solutions. Remember to prioritize compatibility, consult documentation, and maintain security awareness when working with external libraries. As you progress in your RPA development journey, you'll discover even more specialized libraries that empower you to create robust and efficient automation solutions for diverse tasks.

7.3 Automation on Autopilot: Triggering Mojo Scripts with Schedulers

In previous chapters, you explored techniques for building robust Mojo programs for various automation tasks. Now, we delve into scheduling tools, empowering you to automate the execution of your Mojo scripts at specific times or intervals. This allows your RPA solutions to run unattended, maximizing their efficiency and reducing manual intervention.

1. The Value of Scheduled Automation:

-Reduced Manual Work: Eliminate the need to manually trigger your Mojo scripts, freeing up human resources for other tasks.

-Time-Sensitive Tasks: Schedule scripts to run at specific times, ensuring tasks are completed on time (e.g., generating reports at the end of the day).

-Recurring Processes: Automate repetitive tasks that need to run at regular intervals (e.g., downloading daily sales data).

2. Popular Scheduling Tools:

Several operating system-specific or platform-agnostic scheduling tools can be used to trigger Mojo script execution:

-Windows Task Scheduler: Built-in tool on Windows systems for scheduling tasks to run at specific times or intervals.

-cron (Linux/macOS): A command-line utility for scheduling tasks on Unix-based systems.

-Third-Party Schedulers: Tools like Apache Airflow or Quartz Scheduler offer more advanced features for complex scheduling workflows.

3. Integrating Schedulers with Mojo:

The specific method for integrating a scheduler with Mojo programs depends on the chosen scheduler tool. Here's a general approach:

-Configure the Scheduler: Define the schedule (time, interval) for running your Mojo script within the scheduler tool's interface.

-Command to Execute: Specify the command that triggers the execution of your Mojo script. This often involves the path to the Python interpreter followed by the location of your Mojo script file.

-Optional Arguments (Advanced): Schedulers might allow additional arguments to be passed to your Mojo script during execution.

4. Example - Scheduling a Mojo Script with Windows Task Scheduler:

-Open Task Scheduler and create a new task.

-Define the trigger (e.g., Daily at 5:00 PM).

-In the "Actions" tab, specify the action to be "Start a program".

-In the "Program/script" field, enter the path to your Python interpreter (e.g., `C:\Python310\python.exe`).

-In the "Add arguments (optional)" field, enter the path to your Mojo script file (e.g., `C:\Projects\my_automation_script.mojo`).

5. Additional Considerations:

-Error Handling: Consider incorporating error handling mechanisms within your Mojo script to manage potential issues that might arise during scheduled execution.

-Logging: Implement logging within your Mojo script to track its execution and identify any errors or unexpected behavior.

-**Security:** If your Mojo script interacts with sensitive data or systems, ensure proper security measures are in place when scheduling its execution.

6. Summary:

By mastering techniques for scheduling Mojo script execution, you elevate your RPA solutions to a new level of automation. Leverage scheduling tools to ensure your tasks run unattended, on time, and at regular intervals. Remember to consider error handling, logging, and security aspects for robust and reliable scheduled automation. As you progress in your RPA development journey, you'll explore more advanced scheduling features and tools to orchestrate complex automation workflows

7.4 Conquering the Climb: Building Scalable RPA Solutions with Mojo

In previous chapters, you explored techniques for building robust Mojo programs to automate various tasks. Now, we delve into strategies for designing scalable RPA solutions, empowering you to handle increasing workloads and ensure your automation remains effective as your business needs evolve.

1. The Importance of Scalability:

As your automation efforts expand, your Mojo solutions will need to handle more complex tasks, larger data volumes, and potentially even concurrent execution. Building scalable RPA solutions from the ground up ensures they can grow alongside your business requirements.

2. Strategies for Scalable RPA Design:

Modular Code: Break down your automation logic into smaller, reusable functions or modules. This promotes code organization, simplifies maintenance, and allows for easier expansion or modification of specific functionalities.

Code snippet

```
def download_data(url, filename):
  # Download data from the specified URL and save to the filename
  # ... (implementation details)

def process_data(data):
  # Process the downloaded data
  # ... (implementation details)

def upload_results(data):
  # Upload processed data to a specific location
  # ... (implementation details)

# Main program flow
data = download_data("https://www.example.com/data.csv", "data.csv")
processed_data = process_data(data)
upload_results(processed_data)
```

Data Management: Carefully plan how data is handled within your automation scripts. Consider using external databases or data warehouses for storing large datasets, especially when dealing with historical or frequently accessed data. This reduces the burden on your Mojo scripts and improves overall performance.

Event-Driven Architecture (Advanced): For complex scenarios, explore event-driven architectures where tasks are triggered by events (e.g., new data arrival) rather than relying on pre-defined schedules. This can improve flexibility and responsiveness to changing conditions.

3. Best Practices for Maintainability:

-Meaningful Naming: Use descriptive variable and function names that reflect their purpose. This enhances code readability and understanding, especially for future modifications.

-Comments: Add comments to explain the logic behind code sections, particularly for complex parts. This aids future maintenance and collaboration.

-Code Documentation: Consider creating external documentation for your RPA solutions, outlining the functionalities, data flows, and dependencies. This can be especially helpful for onboarding new team members or revisiting code after a long period.

4. Testing and Monitoring:

-Thorough Testing: Test your RPA solutions rigorously under various conditions (different data volumes, network scenarios) to identify potential bottlenecks or scalability issues.

-Monitoring Tools: Utilize monitoring tools to track the performance of your automation processes. This allows you to identify areas for improvement and ensure your RPA solutions are functioning efficiently as workloads increase.

5. Summary:

By prioritizing scalability in your RPA design with Mojo, you ensure your automation solutions can evolve alongside your business needs. Embrace modular code, strategic data management, and maintainability best practices. Leverage testing and monitoring to continually assess and improve the performance of your RPA as your workloads grow. Remember, scalability is an ongoing process, and you'll adapt and refine your automation strategies as your RPA journey progresses.

Chapter 8: Advanced Mojo Programming Techniques

8.1 Mastering the Unexpected: Advanced Exception Handling in Mojo

1. Beyond the Basics:

While the `try-except` block is a fundamental construct, advanced exception handling techniques offer more control and flexibility:

Specific Exception Types: Catch specific exception types (e.g., `FileNotFoundError`, `ConnectionError`) to handle different error scenarios with appropriate actions.

Code snippet

```
try:
  with open("data.txt", "r") as file:
    data = file.read()
except FileNotFoundError:
  print("Error: File not found!")
except Exception as e:  # Catch any other exceptions
  print(f"Unexpected error: {e}")
```

Custom Exceptions: Define your own custom exception classes to represent errors specific to your automation logic. This improves code readability and maintainability.

Code snippet

```
class DownloadError(Exception):
    pass

def download_data(url, filename):
    # Download logic
    if download_failed:
        raise DownloadError("Failed to download data from the specified URL")

try:

download_data("https://www.example.com/data.csv", "data.csv")
except DownloadError as e:
    print(f"Download failed: {e}")
```

Exception Chaining: When raising an exception within an exception handler, you can chain the original exception to the new one. This provides a more detailed error trace for debugging purposes.

Code snippet

```
def process_data(data):
    try:
        # Process data
    except ValueError as e:
        raise RuntimeError("Data processing failed") from e  # Chain the original ValueError
```

```
try:
    process_data(invalid_data)
except RuntimeError as e:
    print(f"Error during data processing: {e}")
    # Access the chained exception using `e.__cause__` if needed
```

2. Advanced Error Handling Strategies:

`finally` **Block:** The `finally` block is always executed after the `try` or `except` block (if an exception occurs). It's commonly used to release resources (e.g., closing files, database connections) regardless of exceptions.

Code snippet

```
try:
    with open("data.txt", "r") as file:
        data = file.read()
except Exception as e:
    print(f"Error: {e}")
finally:
    # Always close the file, even if an exception occurred
    file.close()
```

Logging Errors: Utilize logging libraries to record error details (exception type, message, traceback) in log files. This facilitates debugging and analysis of errors that might occur during script execution.

3. Best Practices for Robust Error Management:

-Handle Expected Exceptions: Anticipate potential errors in your automation workflow and implement specific exception handling for them.

-Don't Swallow Exceptions: Avoid catching exceptions without handling them appropriately. This can mask underlying issues and make debugging difficult.

-Provide Meaningful Error Messages: Strive to provide informative error messages that clearly explain the nature of the error, aiding in troubleshooting and resolution.

4. Summary:

By mastering advanced exception handling techniques in Mojo, you build automation solutions that are resilient to errors and unexpected situations. Leverage specific exception types, custom exceptions, exception chaining, and the `finally` block for comprehensive error management. Remember to prioritize logging errors and follow best practices for robust and maintainable automation code. As you progress in your RPA development journey, you'll explore more advanced error handling strategies and logging frameworks to ensure your RPA solutions can effectively handle even the most complex error scenarios.

8.2 Mastering Patterns: Unleashing the Power of Regular Expressions in Mojo

In previous chapters, you explored techniques for string manipulation and data processing in Mojo. Now, we delve into the world of regular expressions (regex), empowering you to tackle complex pattern matching and data manipulation tasks within your automation scripts.

1. What are Regular Expressions?

Regular expressions are powerful tools for defining patterns within text data. They use a combination of special characters and symbols to represent specific patterns you want to find, extract, or replace within strings.

2. Why Use Regular Expressions?

-Extracting Data: Regular expressions excel at extracting specific information from text (e.g., email addresses, phone numbers, product codes) based on defined patterns.

-Validating Data: Ensure data conforms to a specific format (e.g., email format validation) using regular expressions.

-Replacing Text: Efficiently replace occurrences of text that match a pattern with a different string.

3. Regular Expressions in Mojo:

The `re` module (built-in) provides functionalities for working with regular expressions in Mojo. Here's an overview:

-Defining a Pattern: Use the `re.compile(pattern)` function to create a regular expression object representing the pattern you want to match.

-Matching: Use the `match` or `search` methods of the regular expression object to find matches within a string.

-Extracting Data: Utilize capture groups within your pattern to extract specific parts of the matched text.

-Replacing Text: The `re.sub` function allows you to replace occurrences of a pattern with a different string within a text.

Code snippet

```
import re

# Example: Extracting email addresses
```

```python
email_pattern = r"[\w\.]+@[\w\-]+\.[\w\.]+"   # Pattern for email addresses
text = "Contact us at support@example.com or sales@example.org"

matches = re.findall(email_pattern, text)  # Find all email addresses
for email in matches:
    print(email)

# Example: Validating phone numbers (replace with your specific pattern)
phone_pattern = r"\d{3}-\d{3}-\d{4}"   # Example phone number pattern
phone_number = "123-456-7890"

if re.match(phone_pattern, phone_number):
    print("Valid phone number")
else:
    print("Invalid phone number format")

# Example: Replacing text
text = "The quick brown fox jumps over the lazy dog."
new_text = re.sub(r"dog", "cat", text)  # Replace "dog" with "cat"
print(new_text)
```

4. Important Considerations:

-Regular Expression Complexity: Regular expressions can become complex. Start with simple patterns and gradually increase complexity as needed.

-Testing Thoroughly: Test your regular expressions with various input data to ensure they match and extract information as intended.

-Online Resources: Several online resources and tutorials offer in-depth explanations of regular expressions and their syntax.

5. Summary:

By mastering regular expressions in Mojo, you unlock a powerful tool for text processing and data manipulation within your automation scripts. Utilize regular expressions for extracting information, validating data, and performing complex text replacements. Remember to start with simple patterns, test thoroughly, and leverage online resources for further exploration. As you progress in your RPA development journey, you'll discover even more advanced techniques for using regular expressions to tackle intricate data processing challenges.

8.3 Building Blocks of Automation: Reusable Components and Functions in Mojo

In previous chapters, you explored techniques for building Mojo programs to automate various tasks. Now, we delve into the concept of code reusability and modularity, empowering you to create reusable components and functions that streamline your development process and promote maintainable automation solutions.

1. The Power of Reusability:

-Reduced Code Duplication: By creating reusable functions and components, you avoid writing the same code repeatedly across different scripts. This saves development time and reduces the risk of errors.

- **Improved Maintainability:** Modular code with well-defined functions is easier to understand, modify, and debug. Changes made to a reusable component can propagate throughout your automation suite, improving overall maintainability.

- **Enhanced Organization:** Reusability promotes a more organized codebase, making complex automation projects easier to navigate and manage.

2. Creating Reusable Functions:

- **Modular Design:** Break down your automation logic into smaller, well-defined functions that perform specific tasks.

- **Function Arguments:** Allow your functions to accept arguments that provide flexibility in how they are used within different contexts in your Mojo scripts.

- **Return Values:** Functions can optionally return values, allowing you to capture results or processed data for further use in your main program flow.

Code snippet

```
def download_file(url, filename):
    """Downloads a file from the specified URL and saves it locally."""
    # Download logic using libraries like `requests`
    # Save the downloaded data to the specified filename

def process_data(data):
    """Processes the provided data (replace with your specific logic)."""
    # Data processing logic
    return processed_data
```

```
# Example usage in the main program
data_url = "https://www.example.com/data.csv"
downloaded_file = download_file(data_url, "data.csv")
processed_data = process_data(downloaded_file)

# Use the processed data for further tasks
```

3. Building Reusable Components:

-Object-Oriented Programming (OOP): While Mojo doesn't strictly enforce object-oriented principles, you can leverage classes to encapsulate functionalities and data associated with reusable components.

-Component Structure: Define a class with methods representing the functionalities you want to reuse within your automation scripts.

-Object Instantiation: Create instances of your component class within your main program to leverage its functionalities.

Code snippet

```
class DataProcessor:
  def __init__(self, data):
    self.data = data

  def clean_data(self):
    # Logic to clean the data
    pass

  def transform_data(self):
    # Logic to transform the data
    pass
```

```
# Example usage
data_file = "data.csv"   # Replace with your data source
data_processor = DataProcessor(read_data_from_file(data_file))
cleaned_data = data_processor.clean_data()
transformed_data = data_processor.transform_data()

# Use the cleaned and transformed data
```

4. Additional Considerations:

-Naming Conventions: Adopt consistent naming conventions for functions and components to improve code readability and maintainability.

-Documentation: Consider creating documentation for your reusable components, explaining their functionalities, usage, and any relevant parameters or return values.

-Testing: Thorough testing of your reusable functions and components ensures they work as expected under various conditions.

5. Summary:

By prioritizing code reusability and modularity in your Mojo development, you build a foundation for efficient and maintainable automation solutions. Embrace the creation of reusable functions and components to streamline development, reduce redundancy, and promote well-organized automation code. Remember to follow best practices for naming, documentation, and testing to ensure your reusable components become valuable building blocks for your RPA endeavors. As you progress in your RPA development journey, you'll explore more advanced techniques for building and managing reusable libraries of automation components.

8.4 Mastering the Craft: Best Practices for Efficient Mojo Development

In previous chapters, you explored various techniques for building automation solutions with Mojo. Now, we delve into best practices for writing clean, efficient, and maintainable Mojo code, empowering you to develop high-quality automation scripts that are easy to understand, modify, and scale.

1. The Importance of Best Practices:

Readability: Well-written code is easier for you and others to understand, reducing maintenance effort and facilitating collaboration.

Efficiency: Following best practices can lead to more efficient code that executes faster and utilizes resources optimally.

Maintainability: Maintainable code is easier to modify and adapt as your automation needs evolve.

2. Coding Conventions:

Indentation: Use consistent indentation (typically 4 spaces) to visually represent code blocks and improve readability.

Naming Conventions: Adopt meaningful and descriptive names for variables, functions, and components. Consider using snake_case for variable and function names, and PascalCase for class names.

Line Length: Maintain a reasonable line length (around 80 characters) to avoid horizontal scrolling and enhance readability.

3. Comments and Documentation:

Inline Comments: Use comments to explain complex logic or non-obvious code sections.

Docstrings: Utilize docstrings (triple-quoted strings at the beginning of functions or classes) to document their purpose, parameters, return values, and any specific usage instructions.

External Documentation: For complex automation projects, consider creating external documentation that outlines the overall workflow, component interactions, and data flows within your RPA solution.

4. Maintainability Best Practices:

Modular Design: Break down your automation logic into well-defined functions and components, promoting reusability and reducing code duplication.

Error Handling: Implement robust error handling mechanisms using `try-except` blocks and custom exceptions to gracefully manage unexpected situations.

Meaningful Error Messages: Strive to provide informative error messages that clearly explain the nature of the error, aiding in troubleshooting and resolution.

Testing: Write unit tests for your functions and components to ensure they work as expected under various conditions. Utilize testing frameworks (if available) to automate the testing process.

5. Optimization Techniques:

Profiling: Use profiling tools to identify performance bottlenecks within your code. This helps you focus optimization efforts on the areas that yield the most significant improvements.

Algorithm Selection: Choose appropriate algorithms and data structures for your tasks. Consider time and space complexity when making these decisions.

Leveraging Built-in Functions: Utilize built-in Mojo functionalities and libraries whenever possible to avoid reinventing the wheel and benefit from optimized implementations.

6. Summary:

By adhering to best practices for efficient Mojo development, you elevate the quality and maintainability of your automation code. Embrace clear coding conventions, informative comments and documentation, and modular design principles. Implement robust error handling, write unit tests, and explore optimization techniques where applicable. Remember, efficient Mojo development is an ongoing process, and you'll continuously refine your coding practices as your RPA expertise grows.

Chapter 9: Deploying and Maintaining Your Mojo RPA Solutions

9.1 Sharing the Automation Power: Packaging and Deploying Mojo Robots

1. The Deployment Journey:

Once your Mojo robot is thoroughly tested and ready for production use, you'll need to package it for deployment. This involves creating a distributable package containing all necessary files and dependencies.

2. Packaging Considerations:

Mojo Script: The core of your automation logic, the Mojo script file itself.

External Libraries: If your robot relies on external libraries, ensure they are included in the package or properly installed on the target deployment environment.

Data Files: Any data files required by your robot (e.g., configuration files, reference data) need to be part of the package.

Documentation (Optional): Consider including clear documentation explaining the robot's functionality, usage instructions, and any specific requirements.

3. Deployment Strategies:

The specific deployment strategy depends on your development environment and target deployment infrastructure. Here are some common approaches:

Shared Network Drive: A simple approach for small-scale deployments where the robot package is placed on a shared network drive accessible to authorized users.

Version Control System (VCS): Utilize a version control system (e.g., Git) to manage your robot's code and facilitate deployments. You can push the robot package to a remote repository and pull it on target deployment machines.

Containerization (Advanced): Consider containerization technologies like Docker for packaging your robot and its dependencies into a self-contained unit, ensuring consistent execution across different environments.

4. Security and Access Control:

Sensitive Data: If your robot interacts with sensitive data, ensure proper encryption and access controls are in place on both the development and deployment environments.

User Permissions: Implement mechanisms to restrict access to robot execution based on user roles and permissions.

Logging and Monitoring: Set up logging and monitoring systems to track robot execution and identify potential issues in production.

5. Additional Considerations:

Testing in Production Environment: While thorough testing is crucial before deployment, consider conducting additional testing within the production environment to account for potential configuration differences.

Version Control and Rollbacks: Maintain good version control practices to track changes and facilitate rollbacks if necessary.

Deployment Automation (Advanced): Explore tools for automating the deployment process, especially for large-scale RPA deployments.

6. Summary:

By mastering techniques for packaging and deploying Mojo robots, you empower your organization to leverage the benefits of your automation solutions. Consider the packaging approach, deployment strategy, and prioritize security measures like access control and data encryption. Remember, deployment is an ongoing process, and you'll adapt your strategies based on your specific automation needs and infrastructure. As you progress in your RPA development journey, you'll explore more advanced deployment techniques and tools for managing complex automation deployments.

9.2 Keeping an Eye on the Automation: Monitoring and Logging for Mojo Robots

In previous chapters, you explored techniques for building, deploying, and managing Mojo robots for various automation tasks. Now, we delve into monitoring and logging practices, empowering you to gain insights into your robot's performance, identify potential issues, and ensure the overall health of your RPA deployments.

1. The Importance of Monitoring and Logging:

Visibility into Automation: Monitoring and logging provide valuable insights into your robot's execution, allowing you to track their success rates, execution times, and resource usage.

Proactive Problem Identification: By analyzing logs, you can identify potential issues (errors, exceptions) before they significantly impact your automation processes.

Auditability and Compliance: Logs serve as an audit trail of your robot's activity, which can be crucial for compliance purposes or troubleshooting historical issues.

2. Monitoring Techniques:

Task Schedulers: Many task schedulers used for triggering robot execution offer built-in monitoring functionalities. These can provide information on job completion status, execution times, and error logs.

Custom Monitoring Tools: Develop or leverage custom tools to monitor robot execution. This could involve capturing robot output, execution times, and error messages in a central location for analysis.

3. Logging in Mojo:

-The `logging` **Module:** The built-in `logging` module in Python offers functionalities for implementing logging mechanisms within your Mojo robots.

-Log Levels: Define different log levels (e.g., DEBUG, INFO, WARNING, ERROR) to categorize the severity of logged messages.

-Log Messages: Use the `logging` module functions (e.g., `debug`, `info`, `warning`, `error`) to record messages at specific log levels within your robot code.

Code snippet

```
import logging

# Configure logging (replace with your desired configuration)
logging.basicConfig(filename="robot_log.txt", level=logging.INFO)
```

```
def perform_task():
    # Your robot logic here
    try:
        # ... (task implementation)
    except Exception as e:
        logging.error(f"Error during task execution: {e}")
    else:
        logging.info("Task completed successfully")

# Example usage
perform_task()
```

4. Log Management:

Centralized Log Collection: Consider establishing a central log collection mechanism to aggregate logs from various deployed robots for easier analysis.

Log Rotation: Implement log rotation strategies to avoid log files growing excessively large and consuming storage space.

Log Analysis Tools: Utilize log analysis tools to filter, search, and analyze log data for efficient troubleshooting and performance monitoring.

5. Additional Considerations:

Security: Ensure log messages don't contain sensitive information that could be exposed if logs are intercepted or accessed by unauthorized users.

Log Levels: Balance the verbosity of logs. Too many DEBUG messages can clutter logs, while too few might not provide sufficient information for troubleshooting.

6. Summary:

By implementing effective monitoring and logging practices for your Mojo robots, you gain valuable insights into their execution and overall health of your RPA deployments. Leverage task schedulers' monitoring features, develop custom tools, and utilize the built-in `logging` module in Mojo to capture and analyze robot activity. Remember to establish log management practices for centralized collection, rotation, and analysis. As you progress in your RPA development journey, you'll explore more advanced monitoring and logging tools to gain deeper visibility into the intricate workings of your automation solutions.

9.3 Safeguarding the Automation: Security Best Practices for RPA

In previous chapters, you explored techniques for building, deploying, and monitoring Mojo robots to automate various tasks. Now, we delve into security best practices for RPA implementations, empowering you to safeguard your organization's data and systems while leveraging the benefits of automation.

1. The Security Landscape of RPA:

RPA solutions interact with sensitive data and systems within your organization's IT infrastructure. A security breach in RPA can have significant consequences. Here's why security is paramount:

Elevated Privileges: RPA robots often require elevated privileges to perform tasks, making them attractive targets for attackers if compromised.

Access to Sensitive Data: RPA robots might handle confidential information (e.g., financial data, customer records). Data breaches can occur if proper security measures are not in place.

Integration with Multiple Systems: RPA solutions often integrate with various systems within your organization, increasing the attack surface if vulnerabilities exist.

2. Security Best Practices:

Least Privilege Principle: Grant robots the least privilege necessary to perform their tasks. Avoid granting them unnecessary access to systems or data.

Data Encryption: Encrypt sensitive data at rest and in transit to minimize the risk of exposure in case of a breach.

Regular Patching: Ensure all systems and software used within your RPA environment (including the RPA platform itself) are kept up-to-date with the latest security patches.

Access Control: Implement robust access control mechanisms to restrict access to the RPA platform, robot execution, and configuration.

User Authentication: Enforce strong user authentication protocols (e.g., multi-factor authentication) for accessing and managing RPA solutions.

Network Segmentation: Consider segmenting the network where your RPA robots operate to limit their access to only the resources they require.

Regular Security Audits: Conduct periodic security audits of your RPA environment to identify and address potential vulnerabilities.

Security Awareness Training: Educate users involved in RPA development, deployment, and management about security best practices to minimize human error.

3. Secure Development Practices:

Secure Coding Practices: Follow secure coding practices to minimize vulnerabilities within your robot code. This includes techniques like input validation and proper error handling.

Code Reviews: Implement code review processes to identify potential security issues within your robot code before deployment.

Version Control: Maintain good version control practices for your robot code to facilitate rollbacks if security vulnerabilities are discovered.

4. Monitoring and Logging:

Monitor Robot Activity: Implement monitoring and logging practices to track robot execution and identify suspicious activity.

Log Analysis: Regularly analyze logs to detect potential security incidents or unauthorized access attempts.

5. Summary:

By prioritizing security best practices throughout your RPA development and deployment lifecycle, you create a robust and secure automation environment. Remember, security is an ongoing process. Stay informed about evolving threats and adapt your security measures accordingly. As your RPA program expands, you'll explore more advanced security tools and frameworks to comprehensively safeguard your automation solutions.

9.4 Keeping Track of Changes: Version Control and Collaboration for Mojo Projects

In previous chapters, you explored techniques for building, deploying, and managing Mojo robots. Now, we delve into the world of version control systems (VCS), empowering you to effectively manage code changes, collaborate with others, and maintain a clear history of your automation projects.

1. The Power of Version Control:

Tracking Changes: Version control systems like Git allow you to track all changes made to your Mojo codebase over time. This provides a historical record of your development process.

Collaboration: Multiple developers can work on the same project simultaneously, with version control facilitating merging and resolving conflicts between code versions.

Reverting to Previous Versions: If you encounter issues after making changes, you can easily revert your codebase to a previous stable version.

Branching and Merging: Version control allows you to create branches for experimenting with new features or bug fixes without affecting the main codebase. These branches can then be merged back into the main codebase when ready.

2. Using Git for Mojo Projects:

Git is a popular and powerful VCS widely used for managing software development projects. Here's how you can leverage Git for your Mojo projects:

Initializing a Git Repository: Use the `git init` command within your project directory to create a new Git repository.

Versioning Your Code: Stage and commit your code changes regularly using `git add` and `git commit` commands. Provide meaningful commit messages describing the changes made.

Tracking Remote Repositories: Connect your local Git repository to a remote repository service like GitHub or GitLab for collaboration and backups.

Pushing and Pulling Changes: Use `git push` to upload your committed code to the remote repository and `git pull` to download changes made by others.

Branching and Merging: Utilize `git branch` to create new branches for development, `git checkout` to switch between branches, and `git merge` to integrate changes from different branches.

3. Collaboration with Git:

Shared Repository: Store your Mojo project code in a shared Git repository accessible to all team members working on the automation project.

Code Reviews: Utilize code review features available in Git platforms to review each other's code changes before merging them into the main codebase. This promotes better code quality and collaboration.

Conflict Resolution: Git helps identify and resolve conflicts that might arise when multiple developers modify the same code sections simultaneously.

4. Best Practices for Version Control:

Commit Regularly: Make frequent commits with clear and concise commit messages to maintain a detailed history of your code changes.

Branching Strategy: Develop a branching strategy for your project, defining guidelines for creating and merging branches to maintain a clean and organized codebase.

Regular Backups: In addition to the remote repository, consider creating regular backups of your local codebase for added security and disaster recovery purposes.

5. Summary:

By incorporating version control practices into your Mojo development workflow, you gain a powerful tool for managing code changes, facilitating collaboration, and ensuring the overall health of your automation projects. Embrace Git or a similar VCS to track changes, collaborate effectively, and maintain a clear history of your automation endeavors. As you progress in your RPA development journey, you'll explore more advanced Git functionalities and branching strategies to streamline collaboration within larger development teams.

Chapter 10: The Future of Mojo and RPA

10.1 A Glimpse into the Future: Emerging Trends in RPA.

1. The Rise of Intelligent Automation:

AI-powered RPA: The integration of Artificial Intelligence (AI) with RPA is a significant trend. AI capabilities like machine learning and natural language processing (NLP) are being incorporated into RPA tools. This allows robots to handle more complex tasks that were previously challenging for traditional RPA solutions.

Example: An RPA robot enhanced with NLP can process customer emails, understand their intent, and extract relevant information, automating tasks currently requiring human intervention.

Cognitive Automation: This next-generation approach combines RPA with AI to create "cognitive robots" that can mimic human decision-making capabilities. These robots can learn from experience, adapt to changing situations, and handle unstructured data.

Example: A cognitive robot processing insurance claims can analyze documents, identify patterns, and make automated decisions based on pre-defined rules and learned insights.

2. The Evolving RPA Landscape:

Hyperautomation: This approach combines RPA with other automation technologies like Business Process Management (BPM) and Intelligent Document Processing (IDP) to create a comprehensive automation ecosystem. This allows for automating entire business processes, not just individual tasks.

Low-Code/No-Code Development: The emergence of low-code/no-code development platforms is making RPA more accessible to users with less technical expertise. These platforms allow for building and deploying robots with minimal coding, democratizing RPA development.

Focus on the "Digital Worker": The focus is shifting from automating individual tasks to creating a digital workforce that can collaborate seamlessly with human employees. This involves equipping robots with better communication and problem-solving skills to function effectively within a human-digital workforce.

3. The Impact on RPA Development:

Increased Capabilities: The integration of AI and cognitive automation will broaden the scope of tasks automatable with RPA. Robots will handle increasingly complex tasks, requiring less human intervention.

Improved Efficiency and Accuracy: AI-powered robots can learn and adapt, leading to more efficient automation processes and improved accuracy in task execution.

Focus on Business Value: As RPA evolves, the emphasis will shift towards maximizing business value by automating processes that deliver the most significant ROI (Return On Investment).

Evolving Skillsets: The RPA development landscape will require a new breed of developers with expertise in both automation technologies and AI concepts.

4. Summary:

The future of RPA is bright, fueled by emerging trends like AI integration and cognitive automation. These advancements will lead to more intelligent, adaptable, and powerful automation solutions. As an RPA developer, staying informed about these trends and embracing continuous learning will be crucial to navigate the ever-evolving landscape of automation.

10.2 The Power of Two: AI and RPA - A Synergistic Force

In previous chapters, we explored the future of RPA and the rising trend of intelligent automation. Now, we delve deeper into the integration of Artificial Intelligence (AI) with RPA, unveiling the potential of this powerful combination and the impact it has on automation solutions.

1. AI-Empowered RPA:

Traditional RPA: RPA excels at automating repetitive, rule-based tasks with high accuracy. However, it struggles with tasks requiring complex decision-making, unstructured data processing, or continuous learning.

AI Integration: By incorporating AI capabilities like machine learning and natural language processing (NLP) into RPA tools, robots gain the ability to handle these more intricate challenges.

2. How AI is Transforming RPA:

Advanced Data Processing: AI-powered RPA can analyze large datasets, identify patterns, and extract valuable insights, automating tasks currently requiring human data analysts.

Improved Decision-Making: Robots can leverage machine learning to make data-driven decisions within predefined parameters, reducing human intervention in complex processes.

Unstructured Data Handling: NLP capabilities empower robots to understand and process unstructured data like emails, documents, and social media conversations, automating tasks previously requiring human interpretation.

Enhanced Flexibility and Adaptability: AI allows robots to learn from experience and adapt to changing situations. This enables them to handle unforeseen circumstances and continuously improve their performance.

3. Benefits of AI-powered RPA:

Increased Automation Scope: The combined power of AI and RPA unlocks the potential to automate a broader range of tasks, encompassing more complex processes and unstructured data.

Improved Efficiency and Accuracy: AI-powered robots can make data-driven decisions and adapt to changing situations, leading to more efficient automation and reduced error rates.

Enhanced Productivity: By automating complex tasks previously requiring human intervention, AI-RPA solutions free up human resources for more strategic activities, boosting overall productivity.

Reduced Costs: Automating labor-intensive tasks with AI-powered RPA solutions can lead to significant cost savings within organizations.

4. Challenges and Considerations:

Development Complexity: Building and deploying AI-powered RPA solutions requires expertise in both RPA and AI technologies, which can be a challenge for some organizations.

Data Availability: AI algorithms rely on large datasets for training and effective performance. Ensuring access to high-quality and relevant data is crucial for successful AI-RPA implementations.

Explainability and Transparency: AI decision-making processes can be complex. It's essential to ensure transparency in how AI-powered robots arrive at their decisions, especially for critical tasks.

5. Summary:

The integration of AI with RPA marks a significant step forward in the evolution of automation. AI-powered RPA solutions offer a compelling future for organizations seeking to automate complex processes, improve efficiency, and maximize the value of their automation investments. By acknowledging the challenges and implementing these solutions thoughtfully, organizations can leverage the power of AI-RPA to achieve a more intelligent and productive workforce. As you progress in your RPA development journey, you'll explore the latest advancements in AI and how they can be integrated with RPA to create even more sophisticated automation solutions.

10.3 Your Path to Automation Expertise: Building a Career in RPA

The field of Robotic Process Automation (RPA) is experiencing rapid growth, creating exciting career opportunities for individuals with the right skillsets and interests. Here, we explore various career paths within RPA, resources for learning and development, and how to position yourself for success in this dynamic field.

1. A World of Opportunities:

The RPA industry offers a diverse range of career paths, catering to various skillsets and experience levels. Here are some prominent roles:

RPA Developer: Design, develop, and implement RPA solutions using RPA tools and scripting languages.

RPA Business Analyst: Analyze business processes, identify automation opportunities, and collaborate with developers to translate requirements into technical specifications.

RPA Solution Architect: Design the overall RPA architecture, considering scalability, security, and integration with existing systems.

RPA Project Manager: Lead RPA development projects, manage resources, ensure project timelines are met, and oversee successful deployments.

RPA Support Specialist: Provide technical support for deployed RPA solutions, troubleshoot issues, and ensure smooth operation.

2. Skills for Success:

While specific technical skills vary depending on the chosen career path, some core competencies are essential for success in RPA:

Technical Skills: Proficiency in RPA tools (UiPath, Automation Anywhere etc.), scripting languages (Python, Java), and basic understanding of relational databases (SQL).

Analytical Skills: The ability to analyze business processes, identify inefficiencies, and determine automation feasibility.

Problem-Solving Skills: RPA development involves troubleshooting and resolving technical challenges during implementation.

Communication Skills: Effectively communicate technical concepts to both technical and non-technical audiences.

3. Learning and Development Resources:

RPA Vendor Training: Most RPA tool vendors offer training courses and certifications to help you gain proficiency in their specific platforms.

Online Courses: Numerous online platforms offer comprehensive RPA training courses, often with video lectures, hands-on exercises, and certification preparation.

Books and Articles: Stay up-to-date with the latest trends and best practices by exploring books and articles published on RPA development and implementation.

Industry Certifications: While not mandatory, earning certifications from RPA vendors or industry organizations can validate your skills and enhance your resume.

4. Building Your RPA Portfolio:

Personal Projects: Develop your skills by building personal RPA projects to automate tasks in your daily workflow or explore open-source RPA projects on platforms like GitHub.

Contribute to Open Source: Contributing to open-source RPA projects allows you to showcase your skills to potential employers and gain valuable experience working on real-world automation challenges.

Volunteer Work: Consider volunteering your RPA expertise to non-profit organizations to gain practical experience and build your portfolio.

5. Finding RPA Jobs:

Job Boards: Many job boards now have dedicated sections for RPA positions. Utilize these platforms to search for RPA developer, analyst, or project manager roles.

RPA Vendor Websites: RPA tool vendors often maintain job boards listing opportunities from their partner network for RPA implementation projects.

Networking: Attend industry events, connect with RPA professionals on LinkedIn, and build your network to increase your visibility to potential employers.

6. Summary:

The field of RPA offers a rewarding career path for individuals with a passion for automation and problem-solving. By actively developing your technical skills, business acumen, and communication abilities, you can position yourself for success in this exciting and rapidly growing field. Leverage the plethora of learning resources available, build your portfolio, and network with RPA professionals to navigate your journey towards a fulfilling career in RPA development and implementation. Remember, continuous learning and staying updated with the latest advancements in RPA technology will be crucial for sustained growth within this dynamic domain.

10.4 Keeping Your Mojo Flowing: Staying Up-to-Date with the Latest Advancements

The world of RPA and Mojo is constantly evolving. As a developer, staying informed about the latest features, best practices, and emerging trends is crucial for maintaining your expertise and crafting efficient automation solutions. Here, we explore strategies for staying current with Mojo advancements and resources to fuel your learning journey.

1. The Importance of Staying Updated:

New Features and Improvements: Mojo developers are continuously releasing new features and functionalities to enhance automation capabilities. Staying informed allows you to leverage these advancements in your projects.

Evolving Best Practices: As the field of RPA matures, best practices for code structure, efficiency, and maintainability are constantly refined. Staying updated ensures you're implementing the latest best practices in your Mojo development.

Security Awareness: New security vulnerabilities or exploits might be discovered in Mojo or its dependencies. Staying informed helps you implement appropriate security measures to protect your automation solutions.

2. Strategies for Staying Current:

Official Mojo Resources:

-Mojo Documentation: The official Mojo documentation is a valuable resource, providing detailed information on Mojo functionalities, syntax, and best practices. Make it a habit to consult the documentation regularly, especially when exploring new features. (https://docs.modular.com/mojo/)

-Mojo Blog: The Mojo blog is a platform where developers share insights, announce new features, and discuss best practices. Regularly check the blog for updates and learning opportunities. (https://www.modular.com/max/mojo)

Community Engagement:

-Mojo Forums: Engage with the Mojo developer community on the official forums. Ask questions, share your experiences, and learn from other developers facing similar challenges. (https://github.com/Benny-Nottonson/voodoo)

-Social Media: Follow Mojo on social media platforms like Twitter or LinkedIn to receive updates on new releases, events, and industry trends.

Industry Resources:

-RPA Blogs and Websites: Many RPA blogs and websites feature articles discussing Mojo, its functionalities, and best practices for development. Explore these resources to broaden your knowledge base.

-Online Courses and Tutorials: Consider enrolling in online courses or utilizing tutorials specifically focused on Mojo development. These can provide structured learning paths to enhance your skills.

3. Continuous Learning:

Experimentation: Don't be afraid to experiment with new Mojo features and functionalities as they are released. Explore the capabilities and limitations through personal projects or test environments.

Contribute to the Community: Once you've gained experience, consider sharing your knowledge by contributing to the Mojo forums or creating your own blog posts or tutorials. This not only benefits others but also reinforces your own understanding.

Attend Events: Whenever possible, attend industry conferences or webinars focused on RPA or Mojo specifically. These events offer opportunities to learn from experts, network with other developers, and gain insights into the latest advancements.

4. Summary:

Staying updated with the latest advancements in Mojo programming empowers you to create more efficient, robust, and secure automation solutions. Utilize the official resources, actively engage in the community, and embrace continuous learning to ensure your Mojo development skills remain sharp. Remember, the RPA landscape is constantly evolving, and your dedication to staying informed will be crucial for your success in this exciting field.

www.ingramcontent.com/pod-product-compliance
Lightning Source LLC
Chambersburg PA
CBHW050108230526
45470CB00004B/1739